Orthodox Theological Texts

No. 1. The Orthodox Veneration of Mary the Birthgiver of God
by St. John (Maximovitch) of Shanghai and San Francisco

No. 2. The First-Created Man (The Sin of Adam and Our Redemption)
by St. Symeon the New Theologian

No. 3. The Place of Blessed Augustine in the Orthodox Church
by Fr. Seraphim Rose

THE PLACE OF BLESSED AUGUSTINE
IN THE ORTHODOX CHURCH

One of the earliest representations of Blessed Augustine, from Cefalú Cathedral in Sicily.

The Place of
BLESSED AUGUSTINE
in the Orthodox Church

Fr. Seraphim Rose

ST. HERMAN OF ALASKA BROTHERHOOD
2007

Published with the blessing of His Grace MAXIM,
✚ Bishop of the Western American Diocese
of the Serbian Orthodox Church

Copyright © 1983, 2007 by the
St. Herman of Alaska Brotherhood
First Edition 1983
Second Edition 1996
Third Edition 2007

Address all correspondence to:
St. Herman of Alaska Brotherhood
P. O. Box 70
Platina, California 96076

www.saithermanpress.com

Front Cover: 20th-century icon of Blessed Augustine from Greece.

Publishers Cataloging-in-Publication

Rose, Hieromonk Seraphim, 1934–1982.
    The place of Blessed Augustine in the Orthodox Church / Fr. Seraphim Rose. — 3rd ed. — Platina, Calif. : St. Herman of Alaska Brotherhood, 2007.
    p. ; cm.
    (Orthodox theological texts ; no. 3)
    ISBN: 978-0-938635-12-3
    Includes bibliographical references and index.
    1. Augustine, Saint, Bishop of Hippo. 2. Orthodox Eastern Church—Doctrines. 3. Grace (Theology). 4. Free will and determinism. I. Title. II. Series.
BR65.A9 R67 2007
270.2/092—dc22 0709   2007936304

I myself fear the cold hearts of the "intellectually correct" much more than any errors you might find in Augustine.... I feel in Augustine the love of Christ.

—Fr. Seraphim Rose, from a letter of 1981

O Truth Who art Eternity! and Love Who art Truth! and Eternity Who art Love! Thou art my God, to Thee do I sigh night and day.

—Blessed Augustine, from the *Confessions*

Bishop Augustinos.

✝

The publishers respectfully dedicate this book to
BISHOP AUGUSTINOS (KANTIOTES)
OF FLORINA, GREECE,
a confessing Orthodox hierarch of the latter times,
a zealous inspirer of the faithful,
and a true shepherd who has stood guard against the wolves,
giving his life for his flock,
in the footsteps of Christ,
the Chief Shepherd.

I am the good shepherd: the good shepherd giveth his life for the sheep. But he that is a hireling, and not the shepherd, whose own the sheep are not, seeth the wolf coming, and leaveth the sheep, and fleeth: and the wolf catcheth them, and scattereth the sheep. The hireling fleeth, because he is an hireling, and careth not for the sheep. I am the good shepherd, and know my sheep, and am known of mine. As the Father knoweth me, even so know I the Father: and I lay down my life for the sheep.
—John 10:11–15

St. Ambrose, Bishop of Milan, through whose orations
Blessed Augustine was converted to Christ.
20th-century icon from England.

CONTENTS

Preface *by Fr. Alexey Young* 13
A Brief Life of Blessed Augustine of Hippo 19

Introduction. 25
   I. The Place of Blessed Augustine in the Orthodox
      Church 29
   II. The Controversy over Grace and Free Will 33
   III. The Doctrine of Predestination 43
   IV. Opinions in Fifth-century Gaul 51
   V. Sixth-century Opinion, East and West 61
   VI. The Ninth Century, St. Photius the Great 65
   VII. Later Centuries: St. Mark of Ephesus 69
   VIII. The Opinion of Blessed Augustine in
      Modern Times 75
   IX. A Note on the Contemporary Detractors of
      Blessed Augustine 83

APPENDICES:
   I. Letters of Fr. Seraphim Rose Concerning
      Blessed Augustine 93
   II. The Heart of Blessed Augustine 103
   III. Standard Description of Blessed Augustine. 115
   IV. Service to Blessed Augustine 117

Index. 139

Fr. Seraphim serving Divine Liturgy at an outdoor chapel which he named "Lindisfarne," in honor of the Western Orthodox monastery in Ireland. Bright Week, 1978, St. Herman of Alaska Monastery, Platina, California.

PREFACE

THE LATE HIEROMONK SERAPHIM* was a man of surpassing gentleness and extremely retiring disposition. Although an excellent public speaker and ardent supporter and inspirer of missionary activity, he preferred, in true monastic spirit, the calm silence of his small forest cell on a mountain in northern California. There, working only by candlelight on an old, battered typewriter, he translated and produced some of the most important Orthodox writings available in the English language. He had acquired the spirit of otherworldliness to such an extent that I more than once heard him say, when asked to speak at some important gathering: "This really is not for me." Nonetheless, he of course always forced himself to "speak a word," and his "word" touched hearts and changed lives.

In his personal life he especially shrank from any kind of controversy or disturbance. Whenever passions were likely to be aroused, he wished to be far away. It is ironic, therefore, that this peaceful monk more than once found it necessary to speak out (with the printed word) in defense of an "underdog." An "underdog" was anything or anyone in Church life that he believed was being treated unfairly, uncharitably, arro-

---

* Fr. Seraphim reposed on August 19/September 2, 1982. This preface was written only a month after his repose by his spiritual son, Fr. Alexey Young (now Hieroschemamonk Ambrose).—ED.

gantly, or dishonestly, or made to serve the interest of petty politics.

I remember well that summer day in 1978 when Fr. Seraphim asked me to listen as he read aloud a lengthy essay he was preparing on the subject of Blessed Augustine. Comments about this particular Church Father had been appearing in some publications, the tone of which were often passionately immoderate. No one in the Church had ever before spoken of a Holy Father in this way. It alarmed Fr. Seraphim to see such a worldly and irreverent tone; he saw this as a sign of deep immaturity in Church life today: "We, the last Christians, are not worthy of the inheritance which they (the Holy Fathers) have left us; ... we quote the great Fathers but we do not have their spirit ourselves." He asked for a spirit of humility, lovingness, and forgiveness in our approach to the Fathers of the Church, rather than "using" them in a hard and cold manner that showed disrespect and lack of understanding. "Let the test of our continuity with the unbroken Christian tradition of the past be, not only our attempt to be precise in doctrine, but also our *love* for the men who have handed it down to us." In the words of St. Photius of Constantinople, which Fr. Seraphim quoted, we must reject the errors but "embrace the men." Awareness of this principle must pervade all discussions about the Fathers of the Church.

"The basic question," Fr. Seraphim said to me when he was studying Blessed Augustine, "is, what should be the *Orthodox* approach to controversies?"—for controversies do occur in Church life from time to time, allowed by God for our growth and understanding. As the reader will see for himself, Fr. Seraphim found the answer to this question, and gave it clearly in the balanced and, above all, fair study of Blessed Augustine which follows. The Saint's strengths and weaknesses are examined, the opinions of other Holy Fathers on

Augustine are consulted and given, and, above all, the *spirit* of the man—whom Fr. Seraphim regarded as a true "Father of Orthodox *piety* ... who had a single deeply Christian heart and soul"—is clearly portrayed, perhaps for the first time in the English language.

Fr. Seraphim titled this essay, "The *Place* of Blessed Augustine in the Orthodox Church." He called it this because there are those today who wish to exclude Augustine altogether from the company of Church Fathers—a novel development, to say the least! Some writers boldly—and without justification (other than their own opinion)—call him a "heretic" and unfairly ascribe to him almost every subsequent error of Latin and Protestant Christendom. Fr. Seraphim, on the other hand, wanted nothing more than to give a sense of Orthodox *perspective* to this issue, explaining to those who seemed not to know that Blessed Augustine does indeed have a proper "place" in the Church—not, to be sure, among the great Fathers, but nonetheless a position of well-deserved recognition by other Holy Fathers.

In 1980, Fr. Seraphim wrote, in a memorial article about one of his own spiritual teachers, Ivan Kontzevitch, that "the poverty of the witness of true Christianity increases, the world grows darker, impiety at times already triumphs openly. Good impulses of the soul wither, sometimes without even being born." But in Blessed Augustine one finds an Orthodox Father who is "kin to all those who are clinging to true Christianity, Holy Orthodoxy, in our own days."

So important is this essay on Blessed Augustine that, when his spiritual father, Abbot Herman, visited Mount Athos, he was thanked by the Athonite monks for having published Fr. Seraphim's work. They were anxious that Orthodox Christians today know that Augustine has an important place in Orthodox theology.

THE PLACE OF BLESSED AUGUSTINE

Blessed Augustine was born in Numidia in northern Africa in A.D. 354. His mother, St. Monica, tried to instill in him a love of virtue, but he was insensible to all but his own desires. As an adult he fell into the error of Manicheism but was later converted to Orthodoxy by another Holy Father, St. Ambrose of Milan. Ordained to the priesthood, he was consecrated Bishop of Hippo in 395. For thirty-five years he ruled this African diocese wisely, participating in the great questions of his time and attending the councils of African hierarchs. He wrote at least 1,000 books, of which the *Confessions* and *The City of God* are justly renowned and still read today.

Fr. Seraphim often recommended the *Confessions* to his spiritual children—especially for Lenten reading—and himself reread the book at least once a year. He once told me that he had wept when he first read it because he was so inspired by the deep compunction and purity of Augustine's heart. Long before the recent criticisms of Augustine, Fr. Seraphim felt that the *Confessions* could speak to contemporary Orthodox Christians and help to "soften their hearts" grown cold with pride and passion. As few others had done, Augustine spoke feelingly of the soul's need to free itself from the enticements of the world before it could hope to grasp the things of the spirit. This was precisely Fr. Seraphim's own constant message to others. He understood it because *he had himself experienced it* through his much-suffering monastic labors.

This study of Blessed Augustine's "place" in Orthodoxy is part of Fr. Seraphim's legacy to Orthodox Christians today—a legacy that includes many, many books and articles over the years, and many other books and translations yet to be published. But more than anything else, this essay embodies the principle of respect for that which is holy—a principle rapidly disappearing from 20th century Orthodoxy. May the publication of this essay edify and instruct many thousands of

PREFACE

good-hearted, searching people who understand something of the path which Blessed Augustine traveled, and who have heard his words and been changed:

> "Narrow is the mansion of my soul; enlarge Thou it, that Thou mayest enter in ... for without Thee what am I to myself except a guide to my own downfall?"

Fr. Alexey Young
Repose of St. Sergius of Radonezh
September 25/October 8, 1982

St. Ambrose, Bishop of Milan. 5th-century mosaic from the Chapel of St. Victor "of the Golden Sky," Milan, Italy.

A Brief Life of
BLESSED AUGUSTINE OF HIPPO
A.D. 354–430

THE tremendously instructive and fruitful life of this Western Father of the Church began on November 13, 354, in a small town of Numidia (now Algeria) in northern Africa. His father, Patrick, did not become a Christian until the end of his life, but his mother, St. Monica, blessed her son with the sign of the Cross at his birth and for many years wept and prayed faithfully for his conversion to Christ.

As a youth, Augustine fell into a deeply sinful way of life, patterned after the pagan sensuality of his day. At the age of only 17 he took a concubine and fathered a son. He also possessed a brilliant mind and was easily able to master the pagan learning of his time. At 19 he discovered Cicero and at once conceived an intense longing for truth. But he was also ambitious, and sought to make a name for himself in the academic world. He became a professor of rhetoric in his home town, then moved on to Carthage, and finally took a position in Rome, the capital of the Western empire.

During his time in Carthage Augustine joined the heretical sect of Manichees (followers of the Babylonian, Mani, who had founded a Gnostic type of dualistic religion), bringing a number of his friends with him into this sect. The Manichees led him to despise the Christian Scriptures and regard them as childish fables not to be taken seriously. When he assumed his professorship in Rome, however, he began to see through the

Manichees, whose immorality exceeded even his own. He became disillusioned and withdrew from the sect. He began to feel that his search for truth would fail when he went to Milan in 384 to seek the position of provincial governor. He was now ready for God to act upon him. The Bishop of Milan at that time was the great Holy Father, St. Ambrose. He had once been the governor of northern Italy and was chosen Bishop by popular acclamation. His holy death in 397 produced such an outpouring of faith that five bishops were not enough to baptize the number of converts that appeared the next day desiring the waters of life.

St. Ambrose was a gifted orator and gave homilies regularly in the cathedral. By God's Providence Augustine was present during a whole series of homilies on the subject of Holy Scripture; this prompted him to seriously investigate Christianity—a true answer to his mother's prayers. This, and his almost simultaneous discovery of Plato's exalted *Dialogues,* inspired him to begin living a celibate life. Finally he came to St. Ambrose for Baptism, together with his son, on Great Saturday of the year 387. In the forty-three years that remained to him, he labored diligently in the Lord's vineyard and also saw to the careful tending of his own soul. The story of his conversion, movingly told in the *Confessions* (written ten years after his Baptism) is considered a "masterpiece of introspective autobiography, expressed in the form of a long prayer to God ... exquisitely told."[*]

In 388, Augustine returned to Africa where he was soon ordained a priest by popular demand, and then, in 395, consecrated bishop. All of the writings he produced from this moment on show a special love for and preoccupation with Scripture, but he also composed further philosophical works as

---

[*] Henry Chadwick, *The Early Church* (Penguin Books, 1967), p. 219.

The church in Milan where, it is believed, Blessed Augustine heard St. Ambrose preach and was converted to the Christian faith.

The reliquary in Milan which now houses the relics of Saints Ambrose, Gervasius and Protasius.

well as poems, and polemical, dogmatic, moral and pastoral works, and about 363 sermons and 270 letters—an extensive body of work equalled only by St. John Chrysostom in the East.

As Bishop, Augustine faced and virtually ended the Donatist Schism, already in existence for 85 years, by means of several local Church Councils. The Council of Carthage in 411 also condemned the heresy of Pelagianism and Augustine was clearly recognized as the primary defender of the Orthodox view. Then he turned his attention to the growing problem of the disintegration of the Roman Empire resulting from the sack of Rome by the Goths. Most pagan citizens—and some Christians, too—believed that the fall of the Empire was because the pagan gods had been ignored by Christianity and were angry. To combat this temptation, Augustine spent fourteen years writing the monumental *City of God,* demonstrating that the Church does not exist for empires and governments, but for salvation and the Kingdom of God.

In 426 Augustine retired as bishop but spent his last years in battle with Arianism. On August 28, 430, he died, surrounded by a great concourse of disciples. This man was of such princely heart and mind, and so zealous in the defense of Orthodoxy, that before death he did not fear to review all of his written works, making corrections of errors that had been brought to his attention, and submitting everything to the future judgment of the Church, humbly imploring his readers: "Let all those who will read this work imitate me not in my errors."

Blessed Augustine's message—the message of true Orthodox piety—is one for our times, as he himself wrote in the *Confessions:* "I was slow in turning to the Lord. My life in Thee I kept putting off from one day to the next, but I did not put off the death that daily I was dying in myself. I was in love with the idea of the happy life, but I feared to find it in its true place, and I sought for it by running away from it. I thought that I should be unbearably unhappy if I were deprived of the embraces of a woman, and I never thought of Thy mercy as a medicine to cure that weakness, because I never tried it.... I sent up these sorrowful words: How long? How long?.... *Why not now?*"

These words are as if written for us, the most feeble Orthodox Christians, for we, too, are in love with the "idea of the happy life," and we do not think of God's mercy, which is a medicine for our weaknesses. May we, being inspired by this good and true Father of the Church, step boldly onto the path which leads to salvation, repeating Blessed Augustine's words: "*Why not now?*"

Fresco of Blessed Augustine by Theophanes the Cretan, from the Meteora Monastery of Varlaam, Greece, 16th century.

INTRODUCTION

THIS little study of Blessed Augustine is presented here in book form at the request of a number of Orthodox Christians who read it in its original form in *The Orthodox Word* (nos. 79 and 80, 1978) and found it to have a message for the Orthodox Christians of today. It can make no claim to completeness as a study of the theology of Blessed Augustine; only one theological issue (grace and free will) is treated here in detail, while the rest of the study is chiefly historical. If it has any value, it is in revealing the attitude of the Orthodox Church to Blessed Augustine over the centuries; and in trying to define his place in the Orthodox Church, we have perhaps thrown some light on the problem of being Orthodox in our contemporary world, where the feeling and savor of true Orthodox Christianity are so rarely encountered among Orthodox theologians. While setting forth the Orthodox attitude towards Blessed Augustine, the author has also had in mind to remove him as a "scapegoat" for today's academic theologians and thus to help free us all to see his and our own weaknesses in a little clearer light—for his weaknesses, to a surprising degree, are indeed close to our own.

These weaknesses of ours were vividly brought out for the author not long after the publication of the original study, when he met a Russian, a recent emigrant from the Soviet Union, who had become converted to Orthodoxy in Russia but still understood much of it in terms of the Eastern religious views which he had long held. For him Blessed Augustine also was a kind of scapegoat; he was accused of mistranslating and misunderstanding Hebrew terms, of teaching wrongly about "original sin," etc. Well, yes, one cannot deny that Blessed Augustine applied his over-logicalness to this doctrine also and taught a distorted view of the Orthodox doctrine of ancestral sin—a view, once more, not so much "un-Orthodox" as narrow and incomplete. Augustine virtually denied that man has *any* goodness or freedom in himself, and he thought that each man is responsible for the *guilt* of Adam's sin in addition to sharing its consequences; Orthodox theology sees these views as one-sided exaggerations of the true Christian teaching.

However, the deficiencies of Augustine's doctrine were made by this Russian emigrant into an excuse for setting forth a most un-Orthodox teaching of man's total freedom from ancestral sin. Some one-sided criticisms of Augustine's teaching on original sin even among more Orthodox thinkers have led to similar exaggerations, resulting in unnecessary confusions among Orthodox believers: some writers are so much "against" Augustine that they leave the impression that Pelagius was perhaps, after all, an Orthodox teacher (despite the Church's condemnation of him); others delight in shocking readers by declaring that the doctrine of original sin is a "heresy."

Such overreactions to the exaggerations of Augustine are worse than the errors they think to correct. In such cases Blessed Augustine becomes, not merely a "scapegoat" on which one loads all possible theological errors, justly or unjustly, but something even more dangerous: an excuse for an elitist philosophy of the superiority of "Eastern wisdom" over everything "Western." According to this philosophy, not only Augustine himself, but also everyone under any kind of "Western influence," including many of the eminent Orthodox theologians of recent centuries, does not "really understand" Orthodox doctrine and must be taught by the present-day exponents of the "patristic revival." Bishop Theophan the Recluse,* the great 19th-century Russian Father, is often

---

* Canonized as a saint by the Russian Orthodox Church in 1988.—ED.

especially singled out for abuse in this regard: because he used some expressions borrowed from the West, and even translated some Western books (even while changing them to remove all un-Orthodox ideas) since he saw that the spiritually impoverished Orthodox people could benefit from such books (in this he was only following the earlier example of St. Nicodemus of the Holy Mountain)—our present-day "elitists" try to discredit him by smearing him with the name of "scholastic." The further implication of these criticisms is clear: if such great Orthodox teachers as Blessed Augustine and Bishop Theophan cannot be trusted, then how much less can the rest of us ordinary Orthodox Christians understand the complexities of Orthodox doctrine? The "true doctrine" of the Church must be so subtle that it can "really" be understood only by the few who have theological degrees from the modernist Orthodox academies where the "patristic revival" is in full bloom, or are otherwise certified as "genuinely patristic" thinkers.

Yet, a strange self-contradiction besets this "patristic elite": their language, their tone, their whole approach to such questions—are so very *Western* (sometimes even "jesuitical"!) that one is astonished at their blindness in trying to criticize what is obviously so much a part of themselves. The "Western" approach to theology, the over-logicalness from which, yes, Blessed Augustine (but not Bishop Theophan) did suffer, the over-reliance on the deductions of our fallible mind—is so much a part of every man living today that it is simply foolishness to pretend that it is a problem of *someone else* and not of ourselves first and foremost. If only we all had even a part of that deep and true *Orthodoxy of the heart* (to borrow an expression of St. Tikhon of Zadonsk) which Blessed Augustine and Bishop Theophan both possessed to a superlative degree, we would be much less inclined to exaggerate their errors and faults, real or imagined.

THE PLACE OF BLESSED AUGUSTINE

Let the correctors of Augustine's teaching continue their work if they will; but let them do it with more charity, more compassion, more *Orthodoxy,* more understanding of the fact that Blessed Augustine is in the same heaven towards which we all are striving, unless we wish to deny the Orthodoxy of all those Fathers who regarded him as an Orthodox Saint, from the early Fathers of Gaul through Sts. Photius of Constantinople, Mark of Ephesus, Demetrius of Rostov, to our recent and present teachers of Orthodoxy, headed by Archbishop John Maximovitch.* At the least, it is impolite and presumptuous to speak disrespectfully of a Father whom the Church and her Fathers have loved and glorified. Our "correctness"—even if it is really as "correct" as we may think it is—can be no excuse for such disrespect. Those Orthodox Christians who even now continue to express their understanding of grace and ancestral sin in a language influenced by Blessed Augustine are not deprived of the Church's grace; let those who are more "correct" in their understanding fear to lose this grace through pride.

Since the original publication of this study there has been a Roman Catholic response to it: we have been accused of trying to "steal" Blessed Augustine from the Latins! No: Blessed Augustine has always belonged to the Orthodox Church, which alone has properly evaluated both his errors and his greatness. Let Roman Catholics think what they will of him, but we have only tried to point out the place he has always held in the Orthodox Church and in the hearts of Orthodox believers.

By the prayers of the holy Hierarch Augustine and of all Thy Saints, O Lord Jesus Christ our God, have mercy on us and save us! Amen.

Hieromonk Seraphim
Pascha, 1980

---

* Archbishop John Maximovitch (1896–1966) had been the spiritual mentor of Fr. Seraphim. In 1994 he was canonized by the Russian Orthodox Church Outside of Russia as St. John of Shanghai and San Francisco.—Ed.

I

The Place of Blessed Augustine in the Orthodox Church

By GOD'S PROVIDENCE, in our own times Orthodox Christianity has been returning to the West which departed from it some 900 years ago. At first largely the unconscious work of emigrants from Orthodox lands, this movement has lately been recognized as a great opportunity for inhabitants of the West itself; for some decades this movement of Western converts to Orthodoxy has been increasing and it has now become quite a common phenomenon.

As Orthodoxy has thus gradually been sinking new roots in the West and becoming once again "indigenous" to these lands, among Western converts there has been a natural increase of awareness of the earlier Orthodox heritage of the West, and particularly of the Saints and Fathers of the early Christian centuries, many of whom are in no way inferior to their Eastern counterparts of the same centuries, and all of whom breathe the air and give off the fragrance of the true Christianity which was so tragically lost in the later West. The love and veneration of Archbishop John Maximovitch (†1966) for these Western Saints has especially served to awaken interest in them and facilitate their "reabsorption," as it were, into the mainstream of Orthodoxy.

THE PLACE OF BLESSED AUGUSTINE

With regard to most of the Saints of the West there have been no problems; as their lives and writings have been rediscovered, there has been only rejoicing among Orthodox Christians to find that the full spirit of Eastern Christianity was once so much a part of the West. Indeed, this rediscovery only bodes well for the continued development of a sound and balanced Orthodoxy in the West.

But with regard to a few Western Fathers there have been some "complications," owing especially to some of the dogmatic disputes in the early Christian centuries; the evaluations of these Fathers have differed in East and West, and for Orthodox Christians it is essential to know their significance in *Orthodox* eyes rather than in later Roman Catholic eyes.

The most eminent of these "controversial" Fathers in the West is, without doubt, Blessed Augustine, Bishop of Hippo in North Africa. Regarded in the West as one of the most important Fathers of the Church, and as the paramount "Doctor of Grace," he has always been regarded with some reserve in the East. In our own days, especially among Western converts to Orthodoxy, there have arisen two opposite and extreme views of him. One view, influenced by Roman Catholic opinions, sees rather more importance in him as a Father of the Church than the Orthodox Church has given him in the past; while the other view has tended to underestimate his Orthodox importance, some even going so far as to call him a "heretic." Both of these are Western views, not rooted in Orthodox tradition. The Orthodox view of him, on the other hand, held consistently down the centuries by the Holy Fathers of the East and (in the early centuries) of the West as well, goes to neither extreme, but is a balanced appraisal of him with due credit given both to his unquestioned greatness and to his faults.

In what follows we shall give a brief historical summary of the Orthodox evaluation of Blessed Augustine, emphasizing the attitude of various Holy Fathers toward him and going into details of his controversial teachings only where this is necessary to make clearer the Orthodox attitudes towards him. This historical investigation will also serve to bring out the Orthodox approach to such "controversial" figures in general. Where Orthodox dogmas are directly attacked, the Orthodox Church and her Fathers have always responded quickly and decisively, with correct dogmatic definitions and anathematizations of those who believe wrongly; but where the matter is one (even though on dogmatic subjects) of differing approaches, even of distortions or exaggerations or well-meaning errors, the Church has always had a moderate and conciliating attitude. The Church's attitude toward heretics is one thing; her attitude toward Holy Fathers who happen to have erred in some point or other, is quite another. We shall see this in some detail in what follows.

St. John Cassian the Roman
(ca. A.D. 356–435).
20th-century icon by Sr. Marie-Manoël.
Today, copies of this icon are given to pilgrims
at the Monastery of St. Victor, which St.
Cassian founded in Marseilles, France.

II

The Controversy over Grace and Free Will

THE MOST HEATED of the controversies surrounding Blessed Augustine, both during his lifetime and afterwards, was that of grace and free will. Without doubt, Blessed Augustine was led into a distortion of the Orthodox doctrine of grace by a certain *over-logicalness* which he possessed in common with the Latin mentality, to which he belonged by culture if not by blood. (By blood he was African, and he had something of the emotional "heat" of southern peoples.) The 19th century Russian Orthodox philosopher Ivan Kireyevsky has well summed up the Orthodox view of this point, which accounts for most of the deficiencies of Blessed Augustine's theology. "No single ancient or modern Father of the Church showed such love for the logical chain of truths as Blessed Augustine.... Certain of his works are, as it were, a single iron chain of syllogisms, inseparably joined link to link. Perhaps because of this he was sometimes carried too far, not noticing the inward one-sidedness of his thinking because of its outward order; so much so that, in the last years of his life, he himself had to write refutations of some of his earlier statements."*

---

* "On the Character of European Civilization," in *Complete Works of I. V. Kireyevsky*, vol. 1, in Russian (Moscow, 1911), pp. 188–89.

Concerning the doctrine of grace in particular, the most concise evaluation of Augustine's teaching and its deficiencies is perhaps that of Archbishop Philaret of Chernigov in his textbook of Patrology: "When the monks of Hadrumetum (in Africa) presented to Augustine that, according to his teaching, the obligation of asceticism and self-mortification was not required of them, Augustine felt the justice of the remark and began more often to repeat that grace does not destroy freedom; but such an expression of his teaching changed essentially nothing in Augustine's theory, and his very last works were not in accord with this thought. Relying on his own experience of a difficult rebirth by means of grace, he was carried along by a feeling of its further consequences. Thus, as an accuser of Pelagius, Augustine is without doubt a great teacher of the Church; but in defending the truth, he himself was not completely and not always faithful to the truth."*

Later historians have often emphasized the points of disagreement between Blessed Augustine and St. John Cassian (Augustine's contemporary in Gaul, who in his celebrated *Institutes* and *Conferences* gave for the first time in Latin the full and authentic Eastern doctrine of monasticism and spiritual life; he was the first in the West to criticize Blessed Augustine's teaching on grace); but such historians have often not sufficiently seen the deeper basic agreement between them. Some modern historians (A. Harnack, O. Chadwick) have tried to correct this shortsightedness by showing the supposed "influence" of Augustine on Cassian; and this observation, although it is also exaggerated, points us a little closer to the truth. Probably St. Cassian would not have spoken so eloquently and so in detail on the subject of God's grace if

---

* Archbishop Philaret of Chernigov, *Historical Teaching of the Fathers of the Church,* vol. 3, in Russian (St. Petersburg, 1882), pp. 33–34.

Augustine had not already been teaching his own one-sided doctrine. But the important thing to bear in mind here is that the disagreement between Cassian and Augustine was not one between Orthodox Father and heretic (as was, for example, the disagreement between Augustine and Pelagius), but rather one between two Orthodox Fathers who disagreed only in the details of their presentation of one and the same doctrine. *Both* St. Cassian and Blessed Augustine were attempting to teach the Orthodox doctrine of grace and free will as against the heresy of Pelagius; but one did so with the full depth of the Eastern theological tradition, while the other was led into a certain distortion of this same teaching owing to his overly-logical approach to it.

Everyone knows that Blessed Augustine was the most outspoken opponent in the West of the heresy of Pelagius, which denied the necessity of God's grace for salvation; but few seem to be aware that St. Cassian (whose teaching was given by modern Roman Catholic scholars the most unjust name of "Semi-Pelagianism") was himself a no less fierce enemy of Pelagius and his teaching. In his final work, *Against Nestorius,* St. Cassian closely connects the teachings of Nestorius and Pelagius (both of whom were condemned by the Third Ecumenical Council at Ephesus in 431) and vehemently castigates them together, accusing Nestorius of "breaking out into such wicked and blasphemous impieties that you seem in this madness of yours to surpass even Pelagius himself, who surpassed almost everyone else in impiety" (*Against Nestorius,* V, 2). In this book also St. Cassian quotes at length the document of the Pelagian presbyter Leporius of Hippo wherein the latter publicly recants his heresy; this document, which, St. Cassian states, contains the "confession of faith of all Catholics" as against the Pelagian heresy, was approved by the bishops of Africa (including Augustine) and was probably written by Augustine himself, who was personally responsible for the conversion of Leporius (*Against Nestorius,* I, 5–6). In another passage of the same book (VII, 27), St. Cassian quotes Blessed Augustine as one of his chief Patristic authorities on the doctrine of the Incarnation (but with a qualification that will be mentioned below). Clearly, in defense of Orthodoxy, and in particular against the Pelagian heresy, Cassian and Augustine were on the same side; it was only in the details of their defense that they differed.

The fundamental error of Augustine was his *overstatement* of the place of grace in Christian life, and his *understatement* of the place of free will. He was forced to this exaggeration, as Archbishop Philaret has well said, by his own experience of conversion, joined to the over-logicalness of his Latin mind which caused him to attempt to define this question too precisely. Never, however, did Augustine *deny* free will; indeed, when questioned he would always defend it and censure those who "are extolling grace to such an extent that they deny the freedom of the human will and, what is more serious, assert that on the day of judgment God will not render to every man according to his deeds" (Letter 214, to Abbot Valentinus of Hadrumetum). In some of his writings his defense of free will is no less strong than that of St. Cassian. In his commentary on Psalm 102, for example ("Who healeth all thy diseases"), Augustine writes: "He will heal you, but you must wish to be healed. He heals entirely whoever is infirm, but not him who refuses healing." The very fact that Augustine himself was a monastic Father of the West, founded his own monastic communities for both men and women, and wrote influential monastic Rules, certainly indicates that in actual practice he understood the significance of ascetic struggle, which is unthinkable without free will. In general, therefore, and especially whenever he must give practical advice to Christian

THE CONTROVERSY OVER GRACE AND FREE WILL

strugglers, Augustine does indeed teach the Orthodox doctrine of grace and free will—as well as he can within the limitations of his theological viewpoint.

But in his formal treatises, especially the anti-Pelagian treatises which took up the last years of his life, when he enters upon a logical discussion of the whole question of grace and free will, he is often drawn away into an exaggerated defense of grace which seems to leave little actual place for human freedom. Let us here contrast several aspects of his teaching with the fully Orthodox teaching of St. John Cassian.

In his treatise "On Rebuke and Grace," written in 426 or 427 for the monks of Hadrumetum, Blessed Augustine writes (ch. 17): "Will you dare to say that even when Christ prayed that Peter's faith might not fail, it would still have failed if Peter had willed it to fail? As if Peter could in any measure will otherwise than Christ had wished for him that he might will." There is an obvious exaggeration here; one feels that there is something *missing* from Augustine's description of the reality of grace and free will. St. John Cassian, in his words on the other chief of the Apostles, St. Paul, supplies this "missing dimension" for us: "He says: *And His grace in me was not in vain; but I labored more abundantly than they all, and yet not I, but the grace of God with me* (I Cor. 15:10). When he says *I labored*, he shows the effort of his own will; when he says *yet not I, but the grace of God*, he points out the value of Divine protection; when he says *with me*, he affirms that grace cooperates with him when he is not idle or careless, but working and making an effort" (*Conferences,* XIII, 13). Cassian's position is balanced, giving proper emphasis to both grace and freedom; Augustine's position is one-sided and incomplete, unnecessarily over-emphasizing grace and thus laying his words open to exploitation by later thinkers who did not think in Orthodox terms at all and could thus conceive (as in 17th-century Jansenism) of an "irresistible grace" which man must accept whether he will or not.

A similar exaggeration was made by Augustine with regard to what later Latin theologians were to call "prevenient grace"—the grace that "prevents" or "comes before" and inspires the arousal of faith in a man. Augustine admits that he himself thought wrongly on this subject before his ordination as bishop: "I was in a similar error, thinking that the faith whereby we believe on God is not God's gift, but that it is in us from ourselves, and that by it we obtain the gifts of God, whereby we may live temperately and righteously and piously in this world. For I did not think that faith was preceded by God's grace...but that we should consent when the Gospel was preached to us I thought was our own doing and came to us from ourselves" ("On the Predestination of the Saints," ch. 7). This youthful error of Augustine is indeed Pelagian, and is the result of an over-logicalness in the defense of free will, making it something autonomous rather than something that *cooperates* with God's grace; but he incorrectly ascribes it to St. Cassian (who was also wrongly accused in the West of teaching that God's grace is given in accordance with human merit), and Augustine himself then fell into the opposite exaggeration of ascribing *everything* in the awakening of faith to Divine grace.

The true teaching of St. Cassian, on the other hand, which is the teaching of the Orthodox Church, was something of a mystification to the Latin mind. We may see this in a follower of Blessed Augustine in Gaul, Prosper of Aquitaine, who was the first to attack St. Cassian directly.

It was to Prosper, together with a certain Hilary (not St. Hilary of Arles, who was in agreement with St. Cassian) that Augustine sent his final two anti-Pelagian treatises, "On the Predestination of the Saints" and "On the Gift of Perseverance"; in these works Augustine criticized the ideas of St. Cassian as they had been presented to him in a summary made by Prosper. After Augustine's death in 430, Prosper stepped forth as the champion of his teaching in Gaul, and his first major act was to write a treatise, "Against the Author of the Conferences" (*Contra Collatorum*), also known as "On the Grace of God and Free Will." This treatise is nothing but a step-by-step refutation of St. Cassian's famous thirteenth Conference, where the question of grace is treated in most detail.

From the very first lines it is clear that Prosper is deeply offended that his teacher has been openly criticized in Gaul: "There are some bold enough to assert that the grace of God, by which we are Christians, was not correctly defended by Bishop Augustine of holy memory; nor do they cease to attack with unbridled calumnies his books composed against the Pelagian heresy" (ch. 1). But most of all Prosper is exasperated at what he finds to be a baffling "contradiction" in Cassian's teaching; and this perplexity of his (since he is a faithful disciple of Augustine) reveals to us the nature of Augustine's error.

Prosper finds that in one part of his thirteenth Conference Cassian teaches "correctly" about grace (and in particular about "prevenient grace")—i.e., just like Blessed Augustine. "This doctrine was not at the outset of the discussion at variance with true piety, and would have deserved a just and honorable commendation had it not, in its dangerous and pernicious progress, deviated from its initial correctness. For, after the comparison of the farmer, to whom he likened the example of one living under grace and faith, and whose work he said was fruitless unless he were aided in all things by the Divine succour, he introduced the very Catholic proposition, saying, 'From which it is clearly deduced that the beginning not only of our acts, but also of our good thoughts, is from God; He it is Who inspires in us the beginnings of a holy will and gives us the power and capacity to carry out those things which we rightly desire'... Again, later on, when he had taught that all zeal for virtue required the grace of God, he aptly added: 'Just as all these things cannot continually be desired by us without the Divine inspiration, likewise without His help they can in no way be brought to completion'" (*Contra Collatorum*, ch. 2:2).

But then, after these and similar quotations which do, indeed, reveal St. Cassian as a teacher of the universality of grace no less eloquent than Blessed Augustine (this is why some think he was "influenced" by Augustine), Prosper continues: "At this point, by a sort of inscrutable contradiction, there is introduced a proposition in which it is taught that many come to grace without grace, and that some also, from the endowments of the free will, have this desire to seek, to ask and to knock..." (ch. 2:4). (That is, he accuses St. Cassian of the same error which Blessed Augustine admits that he himself had made in his earlier years.) "O Catholic teacher, why do you forsake your profession, why do you turn to the cloudy darkness of falsity and depart from the light of the clearest truth?... On your part there is complete agreement with neither the heretics nor the Catholics. The former regard the beginnings in every just work of man as belonging to the free will; while we (Catholics) constantly believe that the beginnings of good thoughts spring from God. You have found some indescribable third alternative, unacceptable to both sides, by which you neither find agreement with the enemies nor retain an understanding with us (chs. 2:5, 3:1).

It is precisely this "indescribable third alternative" that is the *Orthodox* doctrine of grace and free will, later to be known by the name of *synergism*, the *cooperation* of Divine grace and human freedom, neither one acting independently or autonomously. St. Cassian, faithful to the fullness of this truth, expresses sometimes the one side (human freedom) and sometimes the other (Divine grace); to Prosper's overly-logical mind this is an "inscrutable contradiction." St. Cassian teaches: "What is it that is said to us, unless in all these (Scriptural quotations) there is a declaration both of the grace of God and the freedom of our will, because even of his own activity a man can be led to the quest of virtue, but always stands in need of the help of the Lord?" (*Conferences,* XIII, 9). "Which depends on which is a considerable problem: namely, whether God is merciful to us because we have presented the beginning of a good will, or we receive the beginning of a good will because God is merciful. Many, believing these individually and affirming more than is right, are caught in many and opposite errors" (*Conferences,* XIII, 11). "For these two, that is, both grace and free will, seem indeed to be contrary to each other; but both are in harmony. And we conclude that, because of piety, we should accept both, lest taking one of these away from man, we appear to violate the Church's rule of faith" (*Conferences,* XIII, 11).

What a profound and serene answer to a question which Western theologians (not only Blessed Augustine) have never been able to answer adequately! To *Christian experience,* and in particular to the monastic experience from which St. Cassian speaks, there is no "contradiction" at all in the cooperation of freedom and grace; it is only human logic that finds the "contradiction" when it tries to understand this question much too abstractly and divorced from life. The very way in which Blessed Augustine, as opposed to St. Cassian, expresses the difficulty of this question, is a revelation of the difference in the depth of their answers. Augustine merely acknowledges that this is "a question which is very difficult and intelligible to few" (Letter 214, to Abbot Valentinus of Hadrumetum), hereby indicating that for him it is a puzzling *intellectual* question; whereas for St. Cassian it is a profound mystery whose truth is known in experience. At the end of his thirteenth Conference St. Cassian indicates that in his doctrine he follows "all the Catholic Fathers who have taught perfection of heart not by empty disputes of words, but in deed and act" (such references to "empty disputes" are the closest he allows himself to come to actual criticism of the eminent Bishop of Hippo); and he concludes this whole Conference on the "synergy" of grace and freedom with these words: "If any more subtle inference of man's argumentation and reasoning seems opposed to this interpretation, it should be avoided rather than brought forward to the destruction of the faith; for how God works all things in us and yet everything can be ascribed to free will cannot be fully grasped by the mind and reason of man" (*Conferences*, XIII, 18).

III

The Doctrine of Predestination

THE MOST SERIOUS of the exaggerations into which Blessed Augustine fell in his teaching on grace is to be found in his idea of *predestination*. This is the idea for which he is most often attacked, and it is the one idea in his works which, when grossly misunderstood, has produced the most frightful consequences in unbalanced minds no longer restrained by the orthodoxy of his thought in general. It should be kept in mind, however, that for most people today the word "predestination" is usually understood in its later Calvinistic meaning (see below), and those who have not studied the question are sometimes inclined to accuse Augustine himself of the same monstrous heresy. It must be stated at the outset of this discussion, then, that Blessed Augustine most certainly did not teach "predestination" as most people understand it today; what he did—as with the rest of his doctrine on grace—was to teach the *Orthodox* doctrine of predestination in an exaggerated way which was easily liable to misinterpretation.

The Orthodox concept of predestination is found in the teaching of St. Paul: *For whom He foreknew, He also predestined to be conformed to the image of His Son...and whom He predestined, them He also called, and whom He called, them He also justified, and whom He justified, them He also glorified*

(Romans 8: 29–30). Here St. Paul speaks of those foreknown and fore-ordained (predestined) by God for eternal glory, it being understood, in the whole context of Christian teaching, that this predestination involves also the free choice of the one being saved; here again we see the mystery of synergy, the co-operation of God and man. St. John Chrysostom writes in his Commentary on this passage (Homily 15 on Romans): "The Apostle here speaks of foreknowledge in order that not everything should be ascribed to the calling.... For if the calling alone were sufficient, then why have not all been saved? Therefore he says that the salvation of the called is accomplished not by the calling alone, but also by foreknowledge, and the calling itself is not compulsory or forcible. Thus, all were called, but not all obeyed." And Bishop Theophan the Recluse explains yet further: "Concerning free creatures, (God's predestination) does not obstruct their freedom and does not make them involuntary executors of His decrees. Free actions God foresees as free; He sees the whole course of a free person and the general sum of all his actions. And seeing this, He decrees as if it had already been accomplished.... It is not that the actions of free persons are the consequence of predestination, but that predestination itself is the consequence of free deeds" (*Commentary on Romans,* chapters 1 to 8, in Russian, Moscow, 1890, p. 532).

However, Augustine's over-logicalness required him to try to look too closely into this mystery and "explain" its seeming difficulties for ordinary logic. (If one is in the number of the "predestined," does he need to struggle for his salvation? If he is not in their number, can he give up struggling altogether?) We need not follow him in his reasonings, except to note that he himself felt the difficulty of his position and found it often necessary to justify himself and qualify his teaching so that it would not be "misunderstood." In his treatise "On the Gift of

THE DOCTRINE OF PREDESTINATION

Perseverance," indeed, he notes: "And yet this doctrine must not be preached to congregations in such a way as to seem to an unskilled multitude, or a people of slower understanding, to be in some measure confuted by that very preaching of it" (ch. 57)—surely a remarkable admission of the "complexity" of basic Christian doctrine! The "complexity" of this doctrine (which, incidentally, is often felt by Western converts to the Orthodox faith, until they have acquired some experience in actual living according to Orthodoxy), resides only in those who have tried to "resolve" it intellectually; the Orthodox teaching of the cooperation of God and man, of the necessity of ascetic struggle, and of the certain will of God that *all* may be saved (I Tim. 2:4), is sufficient to dissolve the unnecessary complications which human logic introduces into this question.

Augustine's intellectualized view of predestination, as he already realized, tended to produce erroneous opinions concerning grace and free will in the minds of some of his hearers. These opinions had apparently become common within a few years of Augustine's death, and one of the great Fathers of Gaul found it necessary to combat them. *St. Vincent of Lerins,* a theologian of the great island monastery off the southern coast of Gaul that was noted for its fidelity to Eastern doctrines in general, and to St. Cassian's teaching on grace in particular, wrote his *Commonitory* in 434 in order to combat the "profane novelties" of various heresies which had been attacking the Church. Among these novelties, he censured the view of one group who "dare to promise in their teaching that in *their* church—that is, in their own small circle—is to be found a great and special and entirely personal form of divine grace; that it is divinely administered, without any pain, zeal, or effort on their part, to all persons belonging to their group, even if they do not ask or seek or knock. Thus, borne up by angels' hands—that is, preserved by angelic protection—they can never *dash their foot against a stone,* that is, they never can be scandalized" (*Commonitory,* ch. 26).

There is another work of this time which contains similar criticisms: *The Objections of Vincent,* which may possibly be the work of the same St. Vincent of Lerins. This is a collection of "logical deductions" from statements of Blessed Augustine which, to be sure, every right-believing Christian would have to oppose: "God is the author of our sins," "repentance is useless for one predestined to death," "God has created the greater part of the human race for eternal damnation," etc.

If the criticisms of these two books were directed against Augustine himself (whom St. Vincent does not mention by name in the *Commonitory*), they are manifestly unfair. Augustine never taught *such* a doctrine of predestination, which simply destroys the whole meaning of ascetic struggle; he himself, as we have seen, found it necessary to come out against those who "are extolling grace to such an extent that they deny the freedom of the human will" (Letter 214), and he would certainly have been on St. Vincent's side against those whom the latter criticized. St. Vincent's criticisms are indeed valid, however, when they are directed (and rightly so) against the immoderate followers of Augustine—those who distorted his teaching in an un-Orthodox direction and, neglecting all of Augustine's explanations, taught that God's grace is effective without human effort.

Unfortunately, however, there is one point of Augustine's teaching on grace, and in particular of predestination, where he fell into a serious error which has given fuel to the "logical deductions" which heretics have made from his doctrine. In Augustine's view of grace and freedom, the Apostle's statement that God *wills all men to be saved* (I Tim. 2:4) cannot be *literally* true; if God "predestines" only some to be saved, then

He must *will* only some to be saved. Here again, human logic fails to understand the mystery of Christian truth. But Augustine, faithful to his logic, must "explain" the passage of Scripture in a way consistent with his whole teaching on grace; and thus he says: "*He wills all men to be saved* is so said that all the predestined may be understood by it, because every kind of man is among them" (*On Rebuke and Grace,* ch. 44). Thus, he does actually deny that God wills all men to be saved. Worse, he is carried so far by the logical consistency of his thought that he even teaches (although only in a few places) a "negative" predestination—a predestination to eternal damnation, something totally foreign to the Scriptures. He speaks clearly of a "class of men which is predestinated to destruction" (*On Man's Perfection in Righteousness,* ch. 13), and again says: "To those whom He has predestinated to eternal death, He is also the most righteous awarder of punishment" (*On the Soul and its Origin,* ch. 16).

But here again we must be careful not to read into Augustine's words the later interpretations of them which Calvin made. Augustine in this doctrine does not at all maintain that God determines or wills any man *to do evil*; the whole context of his thought makes it clear that he believed no such thing, and he often denied this specific accusation, sometimes with evident exasperation. Thus, when it was objected to him that "it is by his own fault that anyone deserts the faith, when he yields and consents to the temptation which is the cause of his desertion of the faith" (as against the teaching that God *determines* a man to desert the faith), Augustine found it necessary to make no reply except: *"Who denies it?"* (*On the Gift of Perseverance,* ch. 46). Some decades later the disciple of Blessed Augustine, Fulgentius of Ruspe, in interpreting this teaching, states: "In no other sense do I suppose that passage of St. Augustine should be taken, in which he affirms that there are certain persons predestinated to destruction, than in regard to their *punishment,* not their sin: not to the evil which they unrighteously commit, but to the punishment which they shall righteously suffer" (*Ad Monimum,* I, 1). Augustine's doctrine of "predestination to eternal death," therefore, does not state that God wills or determines any man to desert the faith or to do evil, nor to be condemned to hell by God's arbitrary will, quite apart from a man's free choice of good or evil; rather, it states that God wills the condemnation of those who, of their own free will, do evil. This, however, is not the Orthodox teaching, and Augustine's doctrine of predestination, even with all its qualifications, is still all too liable to mislead people.

Augustine's teaching was expressed well before St. Cassian wrote his *Conferences,* and it is obvious whom the latter had in mind when, in his thirteenth Conference, he gave the clear Orthodox answer to this error: "For if He willeth not that one of His little ones should perish, how can we imagine without grievous blasphemy that He does not generally will *all* men, but only *some* instead of *all* to be saved? Those then who perish, perish against His will" (*Conferences,* XIII, 7). Augustine would not be able to accept such a doctrine, because he has falsely *absolutized* grace and can conceive of nothing that can happen against the will of God, but in the Orthodox doctrine of synergy, a truer place is given to the mystery of human freedom, which can indeed choose not to accept what God has willed for it and constantly calls it to.

The doctrine of predestination (not in Augustine's restricted sense, but in the fatalistic sense it was given by later heretics) had a lamentable future in the West. There were at least three major outbreaks of it: in the mid-5th century, the presbyter Lucidus taught an absolute predestination both to salvation and damnation, God's power irresistibly impelling some to good and others to evil—although he repented of this doctrine after being combatted by St. Faustus, Bishop of Rhegium, a worthy disciple of Lerins and of St. Cassian, and being condemned by the provincial Council of Arles in about the year 475; in the 9th century, the Saxon monk Gottschalk started the controversy anew, affirming two "absolutely similar" predestinations (one to salvation and one to damnation), denying human freedom as well as God's will to save all men, and thus arousing a violent controversy in the Frankish empire; and, in modern times, Luther, Zwingli, and especially Calvin taught the most extreme form of predestination: that God has created some men as "vessels of wrath" for sin and eternal damnation, and that salvation and damnation are granted by God solely at His pleasure without regard to men's actions. Although Augustine himself never taught anything like these gloomy and most un-Christian doctrines, still the ultimate source of them is clear, and even the Catholic Encyclopedia (1911 edition, which was careful to defend the orthodoxy of Augustine) admits it: "The origin of heretical predestinarianism must be traced back to the misunderstanding and misinterpretation of St. Augustine's views relating to eternal election and reprobation. But it was only after his death that this heresy sprang up in the Church of the West, whilst that of the East was preserved in a remarkable manner from these extravagances" (vol. XII, p. 376). Nothing can be clearer than that the East was preserved from these heresies precisely by the doctrine of St. Cassian and the Eastern Fathers who correctly taught on grace and freedom and left no room for "misinterpretations" of the doctrine.

The exaggerations of Blessed Augustine in his teaching on grace were, therefore, quite serious and had lamentable consequences. Let us not, however, exaggerate ourselves and find him guilty of the extreme views which obvious heretics, as well as his enemies, have ascribed to him. Nor must we place on him all the blame for the arising of these heresies; such a view overlooks the actual nature of the course of intellectual history. Even the greatest thinker does not exert influence in an intellectual vacuum; the reason why extreme predestinarianism broke out at different times in the West (and not in the East) was due first of all, not to Augustine's teaching (which was only a pretext and a seeming justification), but rather to the overly-logical mentality which has always been present in the peoples of the West: in Augustine's case it produced exaggerations in a basically Orthodox thinker, while in the case of Calvin (for example) it produced an abominable heresy in someone who was far indeed from Orthodoxy in thought and feeling. If Augustine had taught his doctrine in the East and in Greek, there would have been no heresy of predestinarianism there, or at least none with the widespread consequences of the Western heresies; the non-rationalistic character of the Eastern mind would not have drawn any consequences from Augustine's exaggerations, and in general would have paid less attention to him than the West did, seeing in him what the Orthodox Church today continues to see in him: a venerable Father of the Church, not without his errors, who ranks rather behind the greatest Fathers of East and West.

But to see this more clearly, now that we have examined in some detail the nature of his most controversial teaching, let us turn to the opinions of the Holy Fathers of East and West with regard to Blessed Augustine.

IV

Opinions in Fifth-Century Gaul

THE OPINION of the Fathers of 5th-century Gaul must be the starting place for this enquiry, for it is there that his teaching on grace was first and most sharply challenged. We have seen the sharpness of the criticism of Augustine's teaching (or that of his followers) by St. Cassian and St. Vincent; how, then, did they and others at this time regard Augustine himself? In answering this question we shall have to touch a little more on the doctrine of grace itself, and also see how the disciples of Augustine themselves were compelled to modify his teaching in answer to the criticisms of St. Cassian and his followers.

Historians of the controversy over grace in 5th-century Gaul have not failed to notice how mild it was in comparison with the disputes against Nestorius, Pelagius, and other obvious heretics; it was always seen as a controversy *within the Church,* not as a dispute of the Church with heretics. Never does anyone call Augustine a heretic, nor does Augustine apply this name to those who criticized him. The treatises written "Against Augustine" are solely the work of heretics (such as the Pelagian teacher Julian), not Orthodox Fathers.

Prosper of Aquitaine and Hilary, in their letters to Augustine informing him of the views of St. Cassian and oth-

THE PLACE OF BLESSED AUGUSTINE

ers (published as Letters 225 and 226 in the works of Augustine), note that although they criticize his teaching on grace and predestination, in other matters they agree with him entirely and are great admirers of his. Augustine in his turn, in publishing his two treatises answering these criticisms, refers to his critics as "those brethren of ours on whose behalf your pious love is solicitous," whose views on grace "abundantly distinguish them from the error of the Pelagians" ("On the Predestination of the Saints," ch. 2). And in the conclusion of his final treatise he offers his opinions humbly to the judgment of the Church: "Let those who think that I am in error consider again and again carefully what is here said, lest perchance they themselves may be mistaken. And when, by means of those who read my writings, I become not only wiser, but even more perfect, I acknowledge God's favor to me" ("On the Gift of Perseverance," ch. 68). Blessed Augustine was certainly never a "fanatic" in his expression of doctrinal disagreements with his fellow Orthodox Christians; and his gracious and generous tone was generally shared by his opponents on the question of grace.

St. Cassian himself, in his book *Against Nestorius,* uses Augustine as one of his eight chief Patristic authorities on the doctrine of Christ's Incarnation, quoting from two of his works (VII, 27). It is true that he refers to Augustine not with words of great praise such as he reserves for Sts. Hilary of Poitiers ("a man endowed with all virtues and graces," ch. 24), Ambrose ("that illustrious priest of God, who never leaving the Lord's hand, ever shone like a jewel upon the finger of God," ch. 25), or Jerome ("the teacher of the Catholics, whose writings shine like divine lamps throughout the whole world," ch. 26). He calls him merely "Augustine the priest (*sacerdos*) of Hippo Regiensis," and there can be little doubt that he does this because he regards Augustine as a Father of less authority than they. Something similar may be seen in the later Eastern Fathers who distinguish between the "divine" Ambrose and the "blessed" Augustine, and this is indeed why Augustine is usually called "blessed" in the East to this day (a name that will be explained below). But the fact remains that St. Cassian did regard Augustine as an authority on a question where his views on grace were not involved—that is, as an Orthodox Father and neither a heretic nor a person whose teaching is dubious or can be disregarded. Similarly, there is an anthology of Augustine's teaching on the Trinity and the Incarnation which has come down to us under the name of St. Vincent of Lerins—another indication that Augustine was accepted as an Orthodox teacher on other questions even by those who opposed his teaching on grace.

Shortly after the death of Blessed Augustine (early 430s), Prosper of Aquitaine made a journey to Rome and appealed for an authoritative opinion from Pope Celestine against those who were criticizing Augustine. The Pope gave no judgment on the dogmatic issues involved, but he did send a letter to the bishops of southern Gaul with what seems to be the prevailing as well as the "official" view of Augustine in the West at that time: "With Augustine, whom all men everywhere loved and honored, we ever held communion. Let a stop be put to this spirit of disparagement, which unhappily is on the increase."

Augustine's teaching on grace did indeed continue to cause disturbance in the Church of Gaul throughout the 5th century. However, the wisest minds on both sides of the controversy spoke moderately. Thus, even Prosper of Aquitaine, the leading disciple of Augustine in the first years after the latter's death, admits in one of his works in defense of him ("Answers to the *Capitula Gallorum,*" VIII) that Augustine spoke too harshly (*durius*) when he said that God did not will that all men should be saved. And his later work (about 450), *The Call*

The original Monastery of St. Roman de l'Aiguille, founded by St. Roman (†460), a disciple of St. John Cassian (†435), as it looks today. Consisting of caves carved out of a mountain, the monastery is located near Beaucaire, France, about sixty miles from the Monastery of St. Victor that St. Cassian founded in Marseilles. *Bottom left:* the bishop's or abbot's seat at the Monastery of St. Roman. *Bottom right:* one of the large rooms.

The necropolis (cemetery) of the Monastery of St. Roman, carved out of the top of the mountain. In the distance on the right is the Rhône River.

of All Nations (*De vacatione omnium gentium*), reveals that his own teaching mellowed considerably before his death. (Some have doubted the traditional ascription of this book to Prosper, but recent scholarship has confirmed his authorship—see the translation of Prosper by de Letter.) This book sets as its aim "to investigate what restraint and moderation we ought to maintain in our views on this conflict of opinions" (Book I, 1), and the author really does try to express the truth of grace and salvation in such a way as to satisfy both sides and put an end to the dispute, if possible. In particular, he emphasizes that grace does not *compel* man, but acts in harmony with man's free will. Expressing the essence of his teaching, he writes: "If we give up completely all wrangling that springs up in the heat of immoderate disputes, it will be clear that we must hold for certain three points in this question. First, we must confess that God wills all men to be saved and to come to the knowledge of truth. Secondly, there can be no doubt that all who actually come to the knowledge of the truth and to salvation, do so not in virtue of their own merits but of the efficacious help of divine grace. Thirdly, we must admit that human understanding is unable to fathom the depths of God's judgments" (Book II, 1). This is essentially the "reformed" (and considerably improved) version of Augustine's doctrine which finally prevailed at the Council of Orange 75 years later and brought an end to the controversy.*

The chief of the Fathers of Gaul after St. Cassian to uphold the Orthodox doctrine of synergy was St. Faustus of Lerins, later bishop of Rhegium (Riez). He wrote a treatise "On the Grace of God and Free Will" in which he attacked both "the pernicious teacher Pelagius" on the one hand, and the "error of predestinarianism" (having in mind the presbyter Lucidus) on the other. Like St. Cassian, he saw grace and freedom as parallel, grace always cooperating with the human will for man's salvation. He compared free will to "a certain small hook" that reaches out and seizes grace—an image not likely to pacify strict Augustinians who insisted on an absolute "prevenient grace." When writing about the books of Augustine in a letter to the deacon Graecus, he notes that even "in the most learned men there are things that may be considered to be suspect"; but he is always respectful to the person of Augustine and calls him *beatissimus pontifex Augustinus*, "the most blessed hierarch Augustine." St. Faustus also kept the feast day of Blessed Augustine's repose, and his writings include a homily for this feast.

---

* See Prosper of Aquitaine, *The Call of All Nations*, trans. P. de Letter, S. J. (Westminster, Maryland: The Newman Press, 1952).

OPINIONS IN FIFTH-CENTURY GAUL

But even the mild expressions of this great Father were found objectionable by strict Augustinians such as the African Fulgentius of Ruspe who wrote treatises on grace and predestination against St. Faustus, and the long-smoldering controversy continued. We may see the Orthodox view of this controversy at the end of the 5th century in the collection of biographical notes of the presbyter Gennadius of Marseilles, *Lives of Illustrious Men* (a continuation of Blessed Jerome's book of the same name). Gennadius, in his treatise *On Ecclesiastical Dogmas,* shows himself to be a disciple of St. Cassian in the question of grace and free will, and his comments on the leading participants in the controversy give us a good idea of how the defenders of St. Cassian in the West regard the question some fifty or more years after the death of both Augustine and Cassian.

About St. Cassian, Gennadius says (ch. 62): "He wrote from experience, and in forcible language, or to speak more clearly, with meaning back of his words and action back of his speech. He covered the whole field of practical directions, for monks of all sorts." There follows a list of his works, with all the Conferences mentioned by name, which makes this one of the longest chapters in the book. Nothing is said specifically of his teaching on grace, but St. Cassian is clearly presented as an Orthodox Father.

About Prosper, on the other hand, Gennadius writes (ch. 85): "I regard as his an anonymous book against certain works of Cassian which the Church of God finds salutary, but which he brands as injurious; and in fact, some of the opinions of Cassian and Prosper on the Grace of God and on free will are at variance with one another." Here the Orthodoxy of Cassian's teaching on grace is specifically declared, and Prosper's teaching is found to be at variance with it; his criticism of Prosper, nevertheless, is mild.

About St. Faustus, Gennadius writes (ch. 86): "He published an excellent work, 'On the Grace of God through Which We Are Saved,' in which he teaches that the grace of God always invites, precedes and helps our will, and whatever gain freedom of will may attain for its pious effect is not its own desert, but the gift of grace." And later, after comments on his other books: "This excellent teacher is enthusiastically believed in and admired." Clearly, Gennadius defends St. Faustus as an Orthodox Father, and in particular defends him against the charge (often made against St. Cassian as well) that he denies "prevenient grace." The followers of Augustine could not understand that the Orthodox doctrine of synergy does not at all deny "prevenient grace," but only teaches its *cooperation* with free will. Gennadius (and St. Faustus himself) made a special point of stating this belief in "prevenient grace."

Now let us see what Gennadius has to say about Augustine himself. It should be remembered that this book was written in the 480s or 490s, when the controversy over Augustine's teaching on grace was some sixty years old, when his exaggerations of the doctrine had been exposed and abundantly discussed, and when the painful consequences of these exaggerations were evident in the already-condemned predestinarianism of Lucidus.

"Augustine of Hippo, bishop of Hippo Regiensis, a man renowned throughout the world for learning both sacred and secular, unblemished in the faith, pure in life, wrote works so many that they cannot all be gathered. For who is there that can boast himself of having all his works, or who reads with such diligence as to read all he has written?" To his praise of Augustine some manuscripts add at this point a criticism: "Wherefore, on account of his much speaking, Solomon's saying came true that *In the multitude of words there wanteth not sin*" (ch. 39). This criticism of Augustine (whether it belongs to Gennadius himself or to a later copyist) is no less mild than

An engraving by Vincent Barralis (1613) of the island of Lerins, where Saints Faustus and Caesarius labored in asceticism.

that of Sts. Cassian and Faustus, merely pointing out that the teaching of Augustine was not perfect. Clearly, the spokesmen of the fully Orthodox teaching on grace in 5th-century Gaul did not regard Augustine as anything but a great teacher and Father, even though they found it necessary to point out his errors. This has continued to be the Orthodox attitude towards Augustine right up to our own day.

By the beginning of the 6th century the controversy over grace had become concentrated in a criticism of the teaching of St. Faustus, whose "little hook" of free will continued to trouble the still overly-logical followers of Augustine. The whole controversy finally came to an end largely through the efforts of one man whose position especially favored a final reconciliation of the two parties. St. Caesarius, Metropolitan of Arles, was an offspring of the monastery of Lerins, where he was the strictest of ascetics, and a follower of the monastic teaching of St. Faustus, whom he never ceased to call a saint; but at the same time he greatly admired and dearly loved Blessed Augustine, and in the end he was to obtain the request he made of God that he might die on the day of Augustine's repose (he died on the eve, August 27, 543). Under his presidency, the Council of Orange was called in 529, with 14 bishops present, and approved 25 canons which gave a somewhat modified version of the teaching of Blessed Augustine on grace. Augustine's exaggerated expressions on the almost irresistible nature of grace were carefully avoided, and nothing whatever was said of his teaching on predestination. Significantly, the doctrine of "predestination to evil" (which some had derived as a mistaken "logical deduction" from Augustine's "predestination to death") was specifically condemned and its followers ("if there are any who wish to believe so evil a thing") anathematized.*

The Orthodox doctrine of St. Cassian and St. Faustus was not quoted at this Council, but neither was it condemned; their teaching of synergy was simply not understood. The freedom of the human will, of course, was maintained, but within the framework of the overly logical Western view of grace and nature. The teaching of Augustine was corrected, but the fullness of the profounder Eastern teaching was not recognized. That is why the teaching of St. Cassian comes today as such a revelation to Western seekers of Christian truth—not that the teaching of Augustine, in its modified form, is "wrong" (for it teaches the truth as well as it can within its limited framework), but that the teaching of St. Cassian is a deeper and fuller expression of the truth.

---

* J. C. Ayer, *A Source Book for Ancient Church History* (New York, 1922), p. 475.

V

Sixth-Century Opinion, East and West

ONCE THE CONTROVERSY over grace had ceased to trouble the West (the East paid little attention to it, its own teaching being secure and not under attack there), the reputation of Augustine remained fixed: he was a great Father of the Church, well known and respected throughout the West, less known but still respected in the East.

The opinion of him in the West may be seen in the references to him by St. Gregory the Dialogist, Pope of Rome, an Orthodox Father recognized in the East as well as the West. In a letter to Innocent, Prefect of Africa, St. Gregory writes (having in mind, in particular, Augustine's commentaries of Scripture): "If you desire to be satiated with delicious food, read the works of the blessed Augustine, your countryman, and seek not our chaff in comparison with his fine wheat" (*Epistles,* Book X, 37). Elsewhere St. Gregory calls him "Saint Augustine" (*Epistles,* Book II, 54).

In the East, where there was little reason to discuss Augustine (whose writings were still little known), the opinion of Blessed Augustine can be most clearly seen on the great occasion in this century when the Fathers of East and West came together—at the Fifth Ecumenical Council, which met at

Constantinople in 553. In the Acts of this Council the name of Augustine is mentioned several times. Thus, during the First Session of the Council, the letter of Emperor St. Justinian was read to the assembled fathers, containing the following passage: "We further declare that we hold fast to the decrees of the Four Councils, and in every way follow the holy Fathers, Athanasius, Basil, Gregory of Constantinople, Cyril, Augustine, Proclus, Leo and their writings on the true faith" (*The Seven Ecumenical Councils,* Eerdmans ed., p. 303).

Again, in the final "Sentence" of the Council, when the fathers invoke the authority of Blessed Augustine on a certain point, he is referred to in this way: "Several letters of Augustine, of most religious memory, who shone forth resplendent among the African bishops, were read..." (ibid., p. 309).

Finally, the Pope of Rome, Vigilius, who had been in Constantinople but had refused to take part in the Council, in the "Decretal Letter" which he issued some months later (while he was still in Constantinople) at last accepting the Council, took as the example for his own retraction Blessed Augustine, whom he spoke about in these terms: "It is manifest that our Fathers, and especially the blessed Augustine, who was in very truth illustrious in the Divine Scriptures, and a master in Roman eloquence, retracted some of his own writings, and corrected some of his own sayings, and added what he had omitted and afterward found out" (ibid., p. 322).

It is evident, then, that in the 6th century Blessed Augustine was a recognized Father of the Church who was spoken about in terms of great praise—praise that was not lessened by recognition of the fact that he sometimes taught imprecisely and had to correct himself.

In later centuries the passage in the letter of Emperor St. Justinian, where he numbers Augustine among the leading Fathers of the Church, was quoted by Latin writers in theological disputes with the East (the text of the Acts of this Council having been preserved only in Latin), with the intention precisely of establishing the authority of Augustine and other Western Fathers in the Universal Church. We shall see how leading Eastern Fathers of these centuries accepted Blessed Augustine as an Orthodox Father, and at the same time handed down to us the correct Orthodox attitude towards Fathers like Augustine who have fallen into various errors.

Fresco of St. Photius the Great from the Sacred Convent
of the Annunciation, Ormylia, Greece.

VI

The Ninth Century: St. Photius the Great

THE THEOLOGY of Blessed Augustine (but no longer his theology of grace) became controversial in the East for the first time late in the 9th century in connection with the famous argument over the *Filioque* (the teaching that the Holy Spirit proceeds "also from the Son" and not from the Father alone, as the East has always taught). This marked the first time that any part of Augustine's theology had been subjected to careful examination by a Greek Father (St. Photius) in the East; the Fathers of Gaul who opposed him on grace, although they taught in the Eastern spirit, all lived in the West and wrote in Latin.

The 9th-century *Filioque* controversy is a vast subject about which an informative book has recently been published.[*] Here we shall only be concerned with the attitude of St. Photius to Blessed Augustine. This attitude is basically the same as that of the 5th-century Fathers of Gaul, but St. Photius gives a more detailed explanation of what the Orthodox view is with regard to a great and holy Father who has erred.

---

[*] Richard Haugh, *Photius and the Carolingians* (Belmont, Massachusetts: Nordland, 1975).

THE PLACE OF BLESSED AUGUSTINE

In one work, his "Letter to the Patriarch of Aquileia" (who was one of the leading apologists for the *Filioque* in the West under Charlemagne), St. Photius answers several objections. To the statement: "The great Ambrose, Augustine, Jerome and certain others have written that the Holy Spirit proceeds also from the Son," St. Photius replies: "If ten or even twenty Fathers have said this, 600 and a numerous multitude have not said it. Who is it that offends the Fathers? Is it not those who, enclosing the whole piety of those few Fathers in a few words and placing them in contradiction to councils, prefer them to the numberless rank (of other Fathers)? Or is it those who choose as their defenders the many Fathers? Who offends holy Augustine, Jerome and Ambrose? Is it not he who forces them to contradict the common Master and Teacher, or is it he who, doing nothing of the sort, desires that all should follow the decree of the common Master?"

Then St. Photius presents an objection typical of the all-too-often narrowly-logical Latin mentality: "If they taught well, then everyone who considers them as Fathers should accept their idea; but if they have not spoken piously, they should be cast out together with the heretics." The answer of St. Photius to this rationalistic view is a model of the depth, sensitivity, and compassion with which true Orthodoxy looks on those who have erred in good faith: "Have there not been complicated conditions which have forced many Fathers in part to express themselves imprecisely, in part to speak with adaptation to circumstances under the attacks of enemies, and at times out of human ignorance to which they also were subject?... If some have spoken imprecisely, or for some reason not known to us, even deviated from the right path, but no question was put to them nor did anyone challenge them to learn the truth—we admit them to the list of Fathers, just as if they had not said it, because of their righteousness of life and

THE NINTH CENTURY: ST. PHOTIUS THE GREAT

distinguished virtue and their faith, faultless in other respects. We do not, however, follow their teaching in which they stray from the path of truth.... We, though, who know that some of our Holy Fathers and teachers strayed from the faith of true dogmas, do not take as doctrine those areas in which they strayed, but we embrace the men. So also in the case of any who are charged with teaching that the Spirit proceeds from the Son, we do not admit what is opposed to the word of the Lord, but we do not cast them out from the rank of the Fathers."*

In his later treatise on the subject of the Procession of the Holy Spirit, the *Mystagogia,* St. Photius speaks in a similar vein regarding Augustine and others who have erred regarding the *Filioque,* and again defends Augustine against those who would falsely make him stand against the Church's tradition, urging the Latins to cover the mistake of their Fathers "using silence and gratitude" (*Photius and the Carolingians,* pp. 151–53).

Blessed Augustine's teaching on the Holy Trinity, like his teaching on grace, missed the mark not so much because it was in error on any specific point; if he had known the full Eastern teaching on the Holy Trinity he probably would not have taught that the Spirit proceeds "also from the Son." He rather approached the whole dogma from a different—a "psychological"—viewpoint that was not as adequate as the Eastern approach in expressing the truth of our knowledge of God; here, as on grace and other doctrines also, the narrower Latin approach is not so much "wrong" as "limited." Several centuries later the great Eastern Father, St. Gregory Palamas, was able to excuse some of the Latin formulations of the Procession of the

---

* *Photius and the Carolingians,* pp. 136–37; some passages added from the Russian translation in Archbishop Philaret of Chernigov, *Historical Teaching of the Fathers of the Church,* vol. 3, pp. 254–55.

Holy Spirit (as long as it was not a matter of the Procession of the *Hypostasis* of the Holy Spirit), adding: "We must not behave in unseemly fashion, vainly quarreling about words."* But even those who taught incorrectly about the Procession of the *Hypostasis* of the Holy Spirit (as St. Photius believed Blessed Augustine had taught), if they taught in this way before the issue was thoroughly discussed in the Church and the Orthodox doctrine was clearly presented to them, are to be treated with leniency and "not cast out from the rank of the Fathers."

Blessed Augustine himself, we should add, was fully deserving of the loving condescension which St. Photius showed in regard to his error. In the conclusion of his book *On the Trinity* he wrote: "O Lord the One God, God the Trinity, whatever I have said in these books that is of Thine, may they acknowledge who are Thine; if anything of my own, may it be pardoned both by Thee and by those who are Thine."

In the 9th century, then, when another serious error of Blessed Augustine was exposed and became a matter of controversy, the Orthodox East continued to regard him as a Saint and a Father.

---

* See Rev. John Meyendorff, *A Study of Gregory Palamas* (London: The Faith Press, 1964), pp. 231–32.

VII

Later Centuries: St. Mark of Ephesus

In the 15th century, at the "Union" Council of Florence, a situation similar to that of St. Photius' time presented itself: the Latins cited Augustine as an authority (sometimes incorrectly) for their teaching on doctrines as various as the *Filioque* and purgatory, and a great theologian of the East answered them.

In their first statement to the Greeks in support of the cleansing fire of purgatory, the Latins brought forward the text of the letter of Emperor St. Justinian to the fathers of the Fifth Ecumenical Council (already quoted above) in order to establish the ecumenical authority in the Church of Blessed Augustine and other Western Fathers. To this St. Mark answered (in his "First Homily on Purgatorial Fire," ch. 7): "First of all you have cited certain words of the Fifth Ecumenical Council which define that in everything one should follow those Fathers whose utterances you intend to quote, and completely accept what they have said; in this number are Augustine and Ambrose who, supposedly, teach more distinctly than others about this cleansing fire. But these words are not known to us, for we do not have the book of Acts of that Council, which is why we request you to present it if you have it written in Greek. For we are quite astonished that in this text Theophilus also is numbered with the other Teachers; he is known everywhere not for any kind of writing, but for an evil renown because of his madness against Chrysostom."*

It is only Theophilus, not Augustine or Ambrose, that St. Mark protests against receiving as a Teacher of the Church. Later in this treatise (chs. 8, 9) St. Mark examines the citations from the "blessed Augustine" and "the divine Father Ambrose" (a distinction which is often retained by Orthodox Fathers in later centuries), refuting some and accepting others. In other writings of St. Mark at this Council he uses the writings of Augustine themselves as an Orthodox source (evidently from the Greek translations of some of his works which had been made after the time of St. Photius). In his "Replies to the Difficulties and Questions of the Cardinals and Other Latin Teachers" (ch. 3), St. Mark quotes from the *Soliloquies* and *On the Trinity*, referring to the author as "blessed Augustine" and using his words effectively against the Latins at the Council (Pogodin, pp. 156–58). In one writing, the "Syllogistic Chapters Against the Latins" (ch. 34), he even refers to "divine Augustine" when again quoting favorably from his *On the Trinity* (Pogodin, p. 268). It should be noted that when St. Mark quotes any Latin teachers who have no authority in the Orthodox Church, he is careful not to give them any title of praise, whether "blessed" or "divine;" thus, Thomas Aquinas for him is only "Thomas, the Latin teacher" (ibid., ch. 13; Pogodin, p. 251).

Like St. Photius, St. Mark, seeing that the Latin theologians were quoting the errors of certain Fathers against the teaching of the Church itself, felt it necessary to state the Orthodox teaching regarding Fathers who have erred on some point. He

---

* Archimandrite Ambrose Pogodin, *St. Mark of Ephesus and the Union of Florence,* in Russian (Jordanville, N.Y., 1963), pp. 65–66. Further references here are to this book, which contains full Russian translations of St. Mark's writings.

does this in a way similar to St. Photius', but with reference not to Augustine—whose errors he tries to justify and place in the best possible light—or to any other Western Father, but to an Eastern Father who fell into an error certainly no less serious than any of Augustine's. Here is what St. Mark writes:

"With regard to the words which are quoted of the blessed Gregory of Nyssa, it would be better to give them over to silence, and not at all compel us, for the sake of our own defense, to bring them out into the open. For this Teacher is seen to be clearly in agreement with the dogmas of the Origenists and to introduce an end to torments." According to St. Gregory (St. Mark continues), "there will come a final restoration of all, and of the demons themselves, 'that God,' he says, 'may be all in all,' as the Apostle says. Inasmuch as these words have also been quoted, among others, at first we shall reply regarding them as we have received it from our Fathers. It is possible that these are alterations and insertions by certain heretics and Origenists.... But if the Saint was actually of such an opinion, this was when this teaching was a subject of dispute and had not been definitely condemned and rejected by the opposite opinion, which was brought forward at the Fifth Ecumenical Council; so that there is nothing surprising in the fact that he, being human, erred in precision (of truth), when the same thing happened also with many before him, such as Irenaeus of Lyons and Dionysius of Alexandria and others.... Thus, these utterances, if they were actually said by the marvellous Gregory concerning that fire, do not indicate a special cleansing [such as purgatory would be—*ed. note*], but introduce a final cleansing and a final restoration of all; but in no way are they convincing for us, who behold the common judgment of the Church and are guided by the Divine Scriptures, but not beholding what each of the Teachers has written as his personal opinion. And if anyone else has written otherwise about a cleansing fire, we have no need to accept it" ("First Homily on Purgatorial Fire," ch. 11; Pogodin, pp. 68–69).

Significantly, the Latins were shocked at this reply and commissioned their leading theologian, the Spanish Cardinal Juan de Torquemada (uncle of the famous Grand Inquisitor of the Spanish Inquisition) to answer for them, which he did in the following words: "Gregory of Nyssa, without doubt most great among Teachers, handed down in clearest fashion the teaching of purgatorial fire ... But what you say in answer to this, that being human he could err, seems to us very strange; for Peter and Paul also, and the other Apostles, and the four Evangelists were likewise human, not to mention that Athanasius the Great, Basil, Ambrose, Hilary and others great in the Church were likewise human and consequently could err! Do you not think that this reply of yours oversteps proper bounds? For then the whole of faith wavers, and the whole of the Old and New Testaments, handed down to us through men, are subjected to doubt, because, if one follows your assertion, it was not impossible for them to err. But what then will remain solid in the Divine Scripture? What will have stability? We also acknowledge that it is possible for a man to err in so far as he is human and does anything by his own powers; but in so far as he is guided by the Divine Spirit and tested by the touchstone of the Church in those things which relate to the common faith of dogmatic teaching, then what is written by him, we affirm, is absolutely true" ("Answering Theses of the Latins," ch. 4; Pogodin, pp. 94–95).

The logical end of this Latin search for "perfection" in the Holy Fathers is, of course, Papal infallibility. The logic of this position is exactly the same as that of those who had protested to St. Photius that if Augustine and others had taught incorrectly on any point they should be "cast out together with the heretics."

LATER CENTURIES: ST. MARK OF EPHESUS

20th-century icon of St. Mark of Ephesus, located at St. Anthony's Greek Orthodox Monastery, Florence, Arizona.

St. Mark, in his new reply to these statements, repeats the Orthodox view that "it is possible for one to be a Teacher and all the same not say everything absolutely correctly, for what need then would the Fathers have had for Ecumenical Councils?"—and such private teachings (as opposed to the infallible

Scripture and Church Tradition) "we must not believe absolutely or accept without investigation." He then goes into great detail, with many citations from his works, to show that St. Gregory of Nyssa actually did teach the error ascribed to him (which is nothing less than the denial of eternal torment in hell, and universal salvation), and gives the final authoritative word on this matter to Augustine himself.

"That only the canonical Scriptures have infallibility is testified by Blessed Augustine in the words which he writes to Jerome: 'It is fitting to bestow such honor and veneration only to the books of Scripture which are called "canonical," for I absolutely believe that none of the authors who wrote them erred in anything.... As for other writings, no matter how great was the excellence of their authors in sanctity and learning, in reading them I do not accept their teaching as true solely on the basis that they thus wrote and thought.' Then, in a letter to Fortunatus [St. Mark continues in his citations of Augustine] he writes the following: 'We should not hold the judgment of a man, even though this man might have been orthodox and had a high reputation, as the same kind of authority as the canonical Scriptures, to the extent of considering it inadmissible for us, out of the reverence we owe such men, to disapprove and reject something in their writing if we should happen to discover that they taught other than the truth which, with God's help, has been attained by others or by ourselves. This is how I am with regard to the writings of other men; and I desire that the reader will act thus with regard to my writings also.'" (St. Mark, "Second Homily on Purgatorial Fire," chs. 15–16; Pogodin, pp. 127–32).

Thus, the last word on Blessed Augustine is that of Augustine himself; the Orthodox Church down the centuries has in fact treated him exactly as he desired.

VIII

Opinion of Blessed Augustine in Modern Times

THE ORTHODOX FATHERS of modern times have continued to regard Blessed Augustine in the same way as did St. Mark, and there has been no particular controversy associated with his name. In Russia, at least as early as the time of St. Demetrius of Rostov (early 18th century), the custom of referring to him as "Blessed Augustine" had become well established. Here let us say just a word about this title.

In the early centuries of Christianity, the word "blessed" with reference to a man of holy life was used more or less interchangeably with the word "saint" or "holy." This was not the result of any formal "canonization"—which did not exist in those centuries—but was based, rather, chiefly on popular veneration. Thus, St. Martin of Tours (4th century), an unquestioned saint and wonderworker, is referred to by early writers such as St. Gregory of Tours (6th century) sometimes as "blessed" (*beatus*) and sometimes as "saint" (*sanctus*). And so, when Augustine is referred to in the 5th century by St. Faustus of Lerins as "most blessed" (*beatissimus*), in the 6th century by St. Gregory the Great as "blessed" (*beatus*) and "saint" (*sanctus*), in the 9th century by St. Photius as "holy" (*agios*), these different titles all mean the same thing: that Augustine was recognized as belonging to the rank of those outstanding for their sanctity and teaching. In the West during these centuries his feast day was kept; in the East (where no special feast would be kept for Western saints) he was simply regarded as a Father of the Universal Church.

By the time of St. Mark of Ephesus the word "blessed" had come to be used for Fathers of somewhat less authority than the greatest Fathers; thus, he refers to "blessed Augustine" but "divine Ambrose," "blessed Gregory of Nyssa" and "Gregory the Theologian, great among the saints"; but he is by no means entirely consistent in this usage.

Even in modern times the word "blessed" remains somewhat vague in its application. In Russian usage "blessed" (*blazhenny*) can refer to great Fathers around whom there has been some controversy (Augustine and Jerome in the West, Theodoret of Cyrus in the East), but also to fools-for-Christ (canonized or uncanonized) and to the uncanonized holy persons of recent centuries in general. Even today there is no precise definition of what "blessed" means in the Orthodox Church (as opposed to Roman Catholicism, where "beatification" is a whole legal process in itself), and any "blessed" person who has a recognized place in the Orthodox calendar of saints (as do Augustine, Jerome, Theodoret, and many fools-for-Christ) could also be called "saint." In Russian Orthodox practice one seldom hears of "Saint Augustine," but almost always of "Blessed Augustine."

In modern times there have been numerous translations of the writings of Blessed Augustine into Greek and Russian, and he has become well known in the Orthodox East. Some of his writings, to be sure, such as his anti-Pelagian treatises and *On the Trinity,* are read only with caution—the same caution with which Orthodox believers read St. Gregory of Nyssa's *On the Soul and the Resurrection* and some other of his writings.

OPINION OF BLESSED AUGUSTINE IN MODERN TIMES

The great Russian Father of the late 18th century, St. Tikhon of Zadonsk, quotes from the writings of Blessed Augustine (chiefly from the *Soliloquies*) as of an Orthodox Father—although of course his main Patristic sources were the Eastern Fathers, and above all St. John Chrysostom.* Augustine's *Confessions* occupied a respected place among Orthodox spiritual books in Russia and even had a decisive effect on the renunciation of the world by the great recluse of the early 19th century, George of Zadonsk. When the latter was in the military service in his youth and was leading an increasingly withdrawn life in preparation for entering a monastery, he was so attracted by a certain colonel's daughter that he had decided to ask her to marry him. Remembering then his cherished desire of abandoning the world, he came to a crisis of indecision and perplexity, which he resolved to end by appealing to the Patristic book he was then reading. As he himself describes this moment: "I was inspired to open the book which lay on the table, thinking to myself: I will follow whatever it opens to at once. I opened the *Confessions* of Augustine. I read: 'He who marries is concerned for a wife, how to please a wife; but he who does not marry is concerned for the Lord, how to please the Lord.' See the rightness of it! What a difference! Reason soundly, choose the better way; do not tarry, decide, follow; nothing hinders you. I decided. My heart was filled with unutterable rejoicing. My soul was in joy. And it seems that my mind was entirely in a heavenly ecstasy."** This experience strongly reminds one of Blessed Augustine's own experience of conversion, when he was inspired to open the Epistles of St. Paul and follow the advice of the first passage on which his

---

* See Nadejda Gorodetzky, *Saint Tikhon of Zadonsk* (Crestwood, N.Y., 1976), p. 118.
** Bishop Nikodim, *Russian Ascetics of the 18th and 19th Centuries,* in Russian (Moscow, 1909), Sept. volume, pp. 542–43.

eyes fell (*Confessions,* VIII, 12). It should be noted that the spiritual world of Blessed George of Zadonsk was entirely that of the Orthodox Fathers, as we know from the books he read: the Lives of Saints, St. Basil the Great, St. Gregory the Theologian, St. Tikhon of Zadonsk, Patristic commentaries on Scripture.

In the Greek Church in modern times the situation has been much the same. The 18th-century Greek theologian Eustratius Argenti, in his anti-Latin works such as the *Treatise on Unleavened Bread,* uses Augustine as a Patristic authority, but he also notes that Augustine is one of the Fathers who fell into some errors—but without thereby ceasing to be a Father of the Church.*

At the end of the 18th century, St. Nicodemus of the Holy Mountain included the Life of Blessed Augustine in his Synaxarion or Collection of Lives of Saints, whereas before this time he had not been included in Eastern calendars and collections of Saints' Lives. This in itself was nothing remarkable; Augustine was but one of many hundreds of names which St. Nicodemus added to the very incomplete Orthodox Calendar of Saints out of his zeal to give greater glory to God's saints. In the 19th century, out of a similar zeal, the Russian Church took the name of Augustine from St. Nicodemus' Synaxarion and added it to its own calendar. This was not any kind of "canonization" of Blessed Augustine, for he had never been regarded in the East as anything other than a Father and a Saint; it was merely a matter of the enlargement of the Church's calendar to make it more complete—a process that is still going on today.

In the 20th century the name of Blessed Augustine is to be found in the standard Orthodox Calendars, usually under the

---

* See Timothy Ware, *Eustratius Argenti* (Oxford, 1964), pp. 126, 128.

date of June 15 (together with Blessed Jerome), but sometimes under the date of his repose, August 28. The Greek Church, as a whole has perhaps regarded him with less reserve than the Russian Church, as may be seen, for example, in the official calendar of one of the "Old-Calendarist" Greek Churches today, where he is called, not "Blessed Augustine" as in the Russian Calendar, but "Saint Augustine the Great" (*agios Augustinos o megas*).

The Russian Church, however, has great love for him, even while not according him the title of "great." Archbishop John Maximovitch, when he became ruling bishop of Western Europe, made it a point of showing special reverence for him (together with many other Western Saints); thus, he commissioned the writing of a special church service in his honor (which until then had not existed in the Slavonic Menaion), and this service was officially approved by the Synod of Bishops of the Russian Church Outside of Russia under the presidency of Metropolitan Anastassy. Archbishop John celebrated this service every year, wherever he might happen to be, on the feast day of Blessed Augustine.*

Perhaps the most balanced critical appraisal of Blessed Augustine in recent times is to be found in the Patrology of Archbishop Philaret of Chernigov, which has been quoted several times above. "He had the very widest influence on his own and subsequent times. But in part he was not understood, in part he himself did not express his thoughts precisely and gave occasion for disputes" (vol. 3, p. 7). "Possessing a logical mind and an abundance of feeling, the Teacher of Hippo did not, however, possess in the same abundance a metaphysical mind; in his works there is much ingenuity but little originality in thought, much logical strictness but not many especially ex-

---

* An English translation of this service is appended to the present book. See pp. 117–38.—ED.

alted ideas. One likewise cannot ascribe to him a thorough theological erudition. Augustine wrote about everything, just like Aristotle, whereas his excellent works could only be and only were his systematic examinations of subjects and his moral reflections.... The highest quality in him is the profound, sincere piety with which all his works are filled" (Ibid., p. 35). Among his moral writings which Archbishop Philaret regards most highly are his *Soliloquies*; his treatises, letters and sermons on monastic struggle and the virtues, on care for the dead, on prayer to the saints, on the veneration of relics; and of course his justly-renowned *Confessions,* "which without doubt can strike anyone to the depths of his soul by the sincerity of their contrition and warm one by the warmth of the piety which is so essential on the path of salvation" (Ibid., p. 23).

The "controversial" aspects of Blessed Augustine's dogmatic writings have sometimes taken up so much attention that this other, moral side of his works has been largely neglected. But his main benefit to us today is probably precisely as a *Father of Orthodox piety*—something with which he was filled to overflowing. Modern scholars, indeed, often find it disappointing that such an "intellectual giant" should have been such "a typical child of his age, even in matters where we should not expect him to be so," that "strangely enough, Augustine fits into a landscape filled with dreams, devils and spirits," and that his acceptance of miracles and visions "reveals a credulity which to us today seems incredible."* Here Blessed Augustine parts company with the "sophisticated" students of theology in our own day; but he is one with the simple Orthodox faithful, as well as with all the Holy Fathers of East and West who, whatever their various failings and differences in

---

* F. Van Der Meer, *Augustine the Bishop* (New York: Sheed and Ward, 1961), p. 553.

theoretical points of doctrine, had a single deeply Christian heart and soul. It is this that makes him unquestionably an *Orthodox* Father and creates an impassable abyss between him and all his heterodox "disciples" of later centuries—but makes him kin to all those who are clinging to true Christianity, Holy Orthodoxy in our own days.

But in many points of doctrine also, Blessed Augustine reveals himself as a teacher for the Orthodox. Especially there should be mentioned his teaching on the Millennium. After being himself attracted to a rather spiritualized form of chiliasm in his earlier years as a Christian, in his mature years he became one of the leading combatters of this heresy which has led astray so many heretics in ancient and modern times who read the *Apocalypse* of St. John in an overly-literal way and not according to the Church's tradition. In the true Orthodox interpretation, which Blessed Augustine taught, the "thousand years" of the *Apocalypse* (ch. 20:1–6) is the whole time from the First Coming to the Second Coming of Christ, when the devil is indeed "bound" (greatly restricted in his power to tempt the faithful) and the saints reign with Christ in the grace-given life of the Church (*City of God,* Book XX, chs. 7–9).

In iconography the features of Blessed Augustine are quite distinctive. Perhaps the earliest surviving icon of him, a 6th-century fresco in the Lateran Library in Rome, is unmistakably based on a portrait from life; the same emaciated, ascetic face and sparse beard appear in a 7th-century icon showing him together with Blessed Jerome and St. Gregory the Great. The icon in an 11th-century manuscript of Tours is more stylized, but still obviously based on the same original. Later Western paintings lose all contact with the original (as happened with most early saints in the West), showing him merely as a medieval or modern Latin prelate.

Above: Blessed Augustine as interpreter of the Psalms. 11th-century manuscript of Tours.

At left: The earliest surviving icon of Blessed Augustine. 6th-century fresco in the Lateran Library, Rome.

IX

A Note on the Contemporary Detractors of Blessed Augustine

ORTHODOX THEOLOGY in the 20th century has been undergoing a "patristic revival." Beyond doubt there is much that is positive in this "revival." Some of the Orthodox textbooks of recent centuries have taught certain doctrines with a partially Western (especially Roman Catholic) vocabulary and slant, and have failed to properly appreciate some of the profoundest Orthodox Fathers, especially of more recent times (St. Symeon the New Theologian, St. Gregory Palamas, St. Gregory the Sinaite). The 20th-century "patristic revival" has at least partially corrected these shortcomings and has freed the Orthodox academies and seminaries of some of the unnecessary "Western influences" that had been present in them. Actually, this has been a continuation of the modern movement of Orthodox self-awareness which was begun in the 18th and early 19th centuries by St. Nicodemus the Hagiorite, St. Macarius of Corinth, Blessed Paisius Velichkovsky, Metropolitan Philaret of Moscow, and others both in Greece and Russia.

But there has been a negative side also of this "patristic revival." For one thing, in the 20th century it has been and remains very largely an "academic" phenomenon: abstract, remote from actual life, bearing the stamp of some of the petty passions of the modern academic world—superiority, smugness, lack of charity in criticizing the views of others, the formation of parties or cliques of those who are "in-the-know" and are aware of which views are "in fashion" and which are not. Some students have such an excessive zeal for the "patristic revival" that they find "Western influence" everywhere they look, become hypercritical of the "Westernized" Orthodoxy of the past several centuries, and have an extremely disdainful attitude towards some of the most respected Orthodox teachers of those centuries (as well as of the present day, and even of antiquity) because of their "Western" views. Little do such "zealots" suspect that they are thus cutting away the Orthodox ground from under their own feet and reducing the unbroken Orthodox tradition to a little "party-line" which a small group of them shares (supposedly) with the "great Fathers" of the past. In this case the "patristic revival" comes perilously close to a kind of Protestantism.*

Blessed Augustine in recent years has become a victim of this negative side of the "patristic revival." The increased *theoretical* knowledge of Orthodox theology in our times (as opposed to the theology of the Holy Fathers, which was inseparably bound up with Christian life) has produced much criticism of Blessed Augustine for his theological errors. Some theological students even specialize in "tearing to pieces" Augustine and his theology, leaving it scarcely possible for one to believe that he can still be a Father of the Church. Sometimes such students come into open conflict with Orthodox theological scholars of the "old school," who in seminary have

---

* For a criticism of one such result of the "patristic revival," see Fr. M. Pomazansky, "The Liturgical Theology of Fr. A. Schmemann," *The Orthodox Word,* no. 35, 1970, pp. 260–80.

been taught some of the defects of Blessed Augustine's theology, but accept him as one Father among many, paying no special attention to him. These latter scholars are closer to the Orthodox opinion of Blessed Augustine down the centuries, while the former are guilty of exaggerating Augustine's faults rather than excusing them (as the great Fathers of the past have done), and in their academic "correctness" often lack that certain inward humility and refinement that mark the authentic transmission of Orthodox tradition from father to son (and not merely from professor to student). Let us look at just one example of this wrong attitude towards Blessed Augustine of some modern students of theology.

An Orthodox priest and professor at a theological school which has experienced the "patristic revival" is giving a lecture on the differences between the mentality of East and West. In discussing the "disastrous distortions of Christian morality" in the modern West, and in particular a false "puritanism" and sense of "perfection," he states: "I cannot trace out the origin of this notion. I only know that Augustine was already introducing it when, if I am not mistaken, he said in his *Confessions* that after his baptism he had no sexual thoughts. I hate to question Augustine's honesty, but it is absolutely impossible for me to accept his statement. I suspect that he made the statement because he already had the notion that since he was a Christian, he was not supposed to have any sexual thoughts. The understanding of Eastern Christianity at the same time was entirely different" (*The Hellenic Chronicle*, Nov. 11, 1976, p. 6). Here Augustine has become, quite simply, a scapegoat on which to pin any views which one finds "un-Orthodox" or "Western"; anything rotten in the West must come from him as its ultimate source! And it is even considered possible, against all laws of fairness, to look into his mind and ascribe to him the most primitive kind of thinking, not to be found even among the freshest converts to Orthodoxy today.

In actual fact, of course, Blessed Augustine never made any such statement. In his *Confessions* he is quite frank in speaking of the "fire of sensuality" which was still in him, and of "how I am still troubled by this kind of evil" (*Confessions* X, 30); and his teaching on sexual morality and the battle against the passions is in general identical with the teaching of the Eastern Fathers of his time—both of which are very different from the modern Western attitude which the lecturer rightly sees as mistaken and un-Christian. (In actual fact, however, the grace of being freed from sexual temptations *has* been given to some Fathers—in the East if not in the West; see *The Lausiac History,* ch. 29, where the ascetic Elias of Egypt, as a result of an angelic visitation, was granted such freedom from lust that he could say, "Passion comes no more into my mind.")

We do not need to be overly harsh ourselves in judging such distortions of the "patristic revival"; so many inadequate and conflicting ideas, many of them truly foreign to the Church, are presented today in the name of Christianity and even of Orthodoxy that one can easily excuse those whose Orthodox views and evaluations are sometimes lacking in balance, as long as it is truly the purity of Christianity that they are sincerely seeking. This very study of Blessed Augustine, indeed, has shown us that precisely this is the attitude of the Orthodox Fathers with regard to those who have erred in good faith. We have much to learn from the generous, tolerant, and forgiving attitude of these Fathers.

Where there are errors, to be sure, we must strive to correct them; the "Western influences" of modern times must be combatted, the errors of ancient Fathers must not be followed. With regard to Blessed Augustine in particular, it cannot be doubted that his teaching missed the mark in many respects:

with regard to the Holy Trinity, grace and nature, and other doctrines; his teaching is not "heretical," but it is exaggerated, and it was the Eastern Fathers who taught the true and profound Christian doctrines on these points.

To some extent the faults of Augustine's teaching are the faults of the Western mentality, which on the whole did not grasp Christian doctrine as profoundly as the East. St. Mark of Ephesus makes a particular remark to the Latin theologians at Ferrara-Florence which might be taken as a summary of the differences between East and West: "Do you see how superficially your teachers touch on the meaning, and how they do not penetrate into the meaning, as for example do John Chrysostom and Gregory the Theologian and other universal luminaries of the Church?" ("First Homily on Purgatorial Fire," ch. 8; Pogodin, p. 66). Some Western Fathers, to be sure, such as Sts. Ambrose, Hilary of Poitiers, Cassian—do penetrate deeper and are more in the Eastern spirit; but as a general rule it is indeed the Eastern Fathers who teach most penetratingly and profoundly of Christian doctrine.

But this in no way gives us grounds for any kind of "Eastern triumphalism." If we boast of our great Fathers, let us beware of being like the Jews who boasted of the very prophets whom they stoned (Matt. 23:29–31). We, the last Christians, are not worthy of the inheritance which they have left us; we are unworthy of even beholding from afar the exalted theology which they both taught and lived; we quote the great Fathers but we do not have their spirit ourselves. As a general rule, it may even be said that it is usually those who cry the loudest against "Western influence" and are the least forgiving of those whose theology is not "pure"—who are themselves the most infected by Western influences, often of unsuspected kinds. The spirit of disparagement of all who do not agree with one's "correct" views, whether on theology, iconography, church services, spiritual life, or whatever subject, has become far too common today, especially among new converts to the Orthodox faith, in whom it is particularly unfitting and often has disastrous results. But even among "Orthodox peoples" this spirit has become too prevalent (obviously as a result of "Western influence"!), as may be seen in the unfortunate recent attempt in Greece to deny the sanctity of St. Nectarios of Pentapolis, a great wonderworker of our own century, because he has supposedly taught incorrectly on some doctrinal points.

Today all we Orthodox Christians, whether of East or West—if only we are honest and sincere enough to admit it—are in a "Western captivity" worse than any our Fathers in the past have known. In previous centuries, Western influences may have produced some theoretical formulations of doctrine that were wanting in preciseness; but today the "Western captivity" surrounds and often governs the very atmosphere and tone of our Orthodoxy, which is often theoretically "correct" but wanting in true Christian spirit, in the indefinable savor of true Christianity.

Let us then be more humble, more loving and forgiving in our approach to the Holy Fathers. Let the test of our continuity with the unbroken Christian tradition of the past be, not only our attempt to be precise in doctrine, but also our love for the men who have handed it down to us—of whom Blessed Augustine was certainly one, as was also St. Gregory of Nyssa, despite their errors. Let us be in agreement with our great Eastern Father, St. Photius of Constantinople, and "not take as doctrine those areas in which they strayed, but *we embrace the men.*"

And Blessed Augustine has something indeed to teach our "precise" and "correct"—but cold and unfeeling—generation of Orthodox Christians. The exalted teaching of the Philokalia is now "in fashion"; but how many who read this book have

A NOTE ON THE CONTEMPORARY DETRACTORS

first gone through the "ABC's" of profound repentance, warmth of heart, and genuine Orthodox piety that shine through every page of the justly-renowned *Confessions* of Augustine? This book, the history of Blessed Augustine's own conversion, has by no means lost its significance today; fervent converts will find in it much of their own path through sin and error to the Orthodox Church, and an antidote against some of the "convert temptations" of our own times. Without the fire of authentic zeal and piety which the *Confessions* reveal, our Orthodox spirituality is a sham and a mockery, and partakes of the spirit of the coming Antichrist as surely as the doctrinal apostasy that surrounds us on all sides.

"The thought of Thee stirs man so deeply that he cannot be content unless he praises Thee; for Thou hast made us for Thyself, and our hearts find no peace until they come to rest in Thee" (Blessed Augustine, *Confessions,* I, 1).

APPENDICES

Fr. Seraphim in 1981, in front of the narthex of the original St. Herman of Alaska Monastery Church, Platina, California.

I

Letters of Fr. Seraphim Rose Concerning Blessed Augustine

✢

Sept. 29/Oct. 12, 1975
St. Cyriacus

Dear Father Igor [Kapral],*

... Now, something at last that is not a request, but an expression of our deep concern over our present-day Orthodox mission. Fr. N—— in his latest *Witness* again makes a self-assured and quite unfounded attack on Blessed Augustine. Everyone knows of the erroneous doctrine of Blessed Augustine on grace—but why this "fundamentalist" attempt to destroy entirely someone who has never in Orthodox tradition been denied a place among the Fathers of the Church? Fr. Theodoritos, doubtless speaking for other zealots in Greece and on the Holy Mountain, writes us that *of course* he accepts Augustine as a Saint, because St. Nicodemus of the Holy Mountain does. Our Vladika John** had a service written to him and had great devotion for him. St. Nikodemos put him in our Eastern Calendar

---

* The future Archbishop Hilarion of Sydney.—Ed.
** St. John (Maximovitch) of Shanghai and San Francisco.—Ed.

(much as Vladika John put St. Patrick there), and our Russian 19th-century Fathers followed him. The Fifth Ecumenical Council ranks Augustine as a theological authority on the same level as Sts. Basil, Gregory and John Chrysostom, with no qualification. The contemporaries of Augustine who disagreed with him (St. Vincent of Lerins, St. John Cassian) corrected his teaching without mentioning his name out of respect, far less calling him a "heretic." His other contemporaries, including great Fathers, always addressed him with the utmost respect. The universal Orthodox tradition accepts him as an undoubted Holy Father, although with a flaw in his teaching—rather like St. Gregory of Nyssa in the East. Whence, then, this strangely "Protestant" campaign to declare Blessed Augustine a heretic, and to utterly condemn anyone who disagrees with this? This greatly disturbs us, not so much for the sake of Blessed Augustine (who, after all, is a Father of less weight than many others), but because it reveals a very unhealthy "party" spirit which threatens the whole English-speaking Orthodox mission. Fr. N—— as much as says: If you do not believe exactly as Fr. P—— believes, you are not Orthodox! If you recommend a 19th-century catechism (as Vladika John always did to converts) you are a Latin; if you read *Unseen Warfare* you are under Latin influence; if you refuse to believe in evolution (!), you are under Western influence!!!

We share our concern with you, because we are really being discouraged by this unhealthy attitude, which is really *zeal not according to knowledge* [Romans 10:2]. We and others have tried gently to communicate with Fr. N—— and Fr. P—— about such things, but the impression is that no communication is possible; on every subject they are "right," they are the "experts," and no other opinion is possible....

Please forgive us for burdening you with all this. We would very much like to know your thoughts with regard to any of this. Is there any way that [they] can be persuaded to be less reckless? There seems to be no one from the "Russians" for whom they have any respect—*everyone* is under "Western influence." (This is Schmemanism!) How can they be made to see, before it is too late, that we should *all* be humble and not think much of our own "theology," that we are *all* perhaps under "Western influences" of various sorts (this is very evident in the case of Fr. N—— himself), but that this should not exclude us from Orthodoxy, as long as we are struggling to understand the truth.

We ask your prayers for us.

With love in Christ,
Seraphim, Monk

✢

March 17/30, 1976
St. Patrick of Ireland

Dear Brother in Christ, Nicholas [Moreno],

Greetings in our Lord Jesus Christ. I pray you are faring well in the Fast and will be prepared to meet the Holy Passion and Resurrection of our Saviour. This is spiritually a very rich part of the year for us, with the long services, the special Lenten tone of life, the readings from the Holy Fathers. I imagine all the readings there are in Russian, but I hope that somehow you are able to get benefit from this practice of readings during the services. Here we have been reading *The Ladder, The Lausiac History,* Abba Dorotheos, and the *Life of the Fathers* [*Vita Patrum*] of St. Gregory of Tours. Reading some of these books over again every year only puts them deeper into one's Orthodox consciousness, and there are always "new" things there no matter how often one has read them—which, of course, only shows how dense we are and how much we need such things.

I hope that in the midst of your learning (which we pray may be very fruitful!) you are also getting the feel for that which can't be directly taught—the tone of Orthodox life and thought which comes "between the lines" as it were, the respect for the older generation which is handing down the sacred treasure of Orthodoxy, the approach to the teaching of the Holy Fathers which should be not academic but practical, and should see beyond superficial "disputes" to the deeper meaning of the Patristic teaching. The Patristic "experts" of the newer school miss this, and this is a great temptation in our Church now also, since everyone is now affected to some degree or other by the soul-less academic air around us. Of late we have noticed how shallow has been the discussion of Blessed Augustine—a cold, calculating approach to him which would either condescendingly "accept" him or else "throw him out of the calendar" based solely on an abstract analysis of his teaching. But the true Orthodox perspective is, first of all, to *distrust* one's abstract "theological" outlook and ask: what do our elders think; what did the recent Fathers think? And taking these opinions respectfully, one then begins to put together the picture for oneself. But the "new theologians," when they hear that our recent fathers such as St. Nicodemus of the Holy Mountain or our own Archbishop John had great respect for Blessed Augustine, can only say with disdain—"they were under Western influence"—and throw out their weighty opinions with a quite "Western" lack of feeling and understanding. Anyone who has read Blessed Augustine's *Confessions* with sympathy will not readily want to "throw him out of the calendar"—for he will see in this book precisely that fiery zeal and love which is *precisely* what is so lacking in our Orthodox life today! Have you read this book, by the way?—you should.

Archbishop Philaret of Chernigov, in his 19th-century Patrology, while setting forth clearly Blessed Augustine's mistakes—or rather, overemphases—still highly praises this book for its warmth and piety. And perhaps Blessed Augustine's very "Westernness" makes him more relevant for us today who are submerged in the West and its way of thought; it is surely pride for us to think that we will read only the great "Eastern" and "mystical" books.

Well, I didn't really mean to digress so much on this subject. But at least you know that we are thinking of you and are very anxious for you to get the maximum from your seminary and monastery experience. Above all, keep your heart open and learn to be a little detached from the many intellectual arguments and currents that buzz about our Church. Let us know how you are doing. Pray for us—we have started to print the book on the Life of Blessed Paisius, which is an immense project for us....

With love in Christ,
Seraphim, Monk

☩

June 13/26, 1981
St. Tryphillius of Cyprus

Dear Father Michael [Azkoul],

Christ is in our midst!

Thank you for your letter. I am frankly happy to see someone with your views on Blessed Augustine willing to do something besides hit him (and all of us who have any respect for him) over the head.

You ask for cooperation on what seems to be a "thorough study" of Blessed Augustine. I really wonder about the value of such a study—for someone who wishes to expose the source of

"Western influence" in Orthodox theology, this detailed analysis itself seems so terribly Western!

If your attempt is to find out Augustine's real place in the Orthodox Church, I think your approach is all wrong. It assumes that "we moderns" are the ones who can do this—that we can "know better" than anyone in the Orthodox past. I don't think so. I have a deep distrust of *all* of us who are writing on theological subjects today—we are more under "Western influence" than anyone before, and the less we are aware of it the more obnoxious our "Westernism" becomes. Our whole cold, academic, and often disdainful approach to theology is so remote from the Fathers, so foreign to them. Let us admit this and try not to be so presumptuous (I speak for myself also).

I have no time (and probably not the sources) to find out how much St. Photios or St. Mark read of Blessed Augustine. I would suspect that St. Photios had read rather little apart from the texts under dispute, and St. Mark probably more (in fact, St. Mark can probably be shown to be under Augustine's "influence" in some way if you search hard enough!—his disciple Gennadius, after all, was the translator of Thomas Aquinas into Greek). Undoubtedly their respect for Augustine was based on the general respect for him in the Church, especially in the West from the very beginning.

And this brings up the only real question I think you might fruitfully research: what did the Western Church think of Blessed Augustine in the centuries when it was Orthodox? The West knew him as one of their own Fathers; it knew his writings well, including the disputes over them. What did the Western Fathers who were linked with the East think of him? We know St. Cassian's opinion—he challenged (politely) Augustine's teaching on grace while accepting his authority on other questions. St. Vincent of Lerins' argument is more with the immoderate followers of Augustine. In neither case was there talk of "heresy," or of someone who was totally un-Orthodox. St. Faustus of Lerins—if anyone, he should be an enemy of Augustine, but the evidence seems to the contrary. St. Caesarius of Arles, St. Gregory the Great—admirers of Augustine, while not following his exaggerations on grace. I don't mention some of the enthusiastic followers of Augustine.

There is room for research here in Latin sources, but no research can overthrow the obvious fact (it seems to me)—the Orthodox West accepted him as a Father. If he's really a "heretic," then doesn't the whole West go down the drain with him? I'm sure you can find enough signs of "Western mentality" in Gregory the Great, for example, to disqualify him as a Father and Saint in the eyes of many of today's Orthodox scholars—he also is accepted in the East on the basis of his general reputation in the West, and on the basis of his "Dialogues" (which I'm sure a few would now question as having a right to be called an Orthodox book).

I think the "heresy hunt" over Augustine reveals at least two major faults in today's Orthodox scholars who are pursuing it:

1. A profound insecurity over their own Orthodoxy, born of the uncertainties of our times, the betrayal of ecumenism, and their own purely Western education. Here Augustine is a "scapegoat"—hit him hard enough and it proves how Orthodox you yourself really are!

2. An incipient sectarian consciousness—in attacking Augustine so bitterly one not only attacks the whole Orthodox West of the early centuries, but also a great many Orthodox thinkers of recent centuries and today. I could name you bishops in our Church who think like Augustine on a number of points—are they, then, "heretics" too? I think some of our anti-Augustinians are coming close to this conclusion, and

THE PLACE OF BLESSED AUGUSTINE

thus close to schism and the formation of an "Orthodox" sect *that prides itself on the correctness of its intellectual views....*

I myself am no great admirer of Augustine's doctrines. He does indeed have that Western "super-logicalness" which the Eastern Fathers don't have (the same "super-logicalness" which the critics of Augustine today display so abundantly!). The one main lovable and Orthodox thing about him is his Orthodox *feeling, piety, love for Christ,* which comes out so strongly in his non-dogmatic works like the *Confessions* (the Russian Fathers also love the *Soliloquies*). To destroy Augustine, as today's critics are trying to do, is to help to destroy also this piety and love for Christ—these are too "simple" for today's intellectuals (even though they also claim to be "pious" in their own way). Today it is Augustine; tomorrow (and it's already begun) the attack will be on the "simple" bishops and priests of our Church. The anti-Augustine movement is a step towards schism and further disorders in the Orthodox Church.

Let us assume that one's exegesis of Romans 5:12 is incorrect; that one believes like Augustine on the transmission of original sin; that one knows little of the difference between the "transcendent" and the "economic" Trinity and sometimes confuses them. Can't one still be Orthodox? Does one have to shout so loudly one's "correctness" on such matters, and one's disdain (and this disdain is strongly felt!) for those who believe thus? In the history of the Church, opinions such as these which disagree with the consensus of the Church have not been a cause for heresy hunts. Recognizing our fallible human nature, the Fathers of the past have kept the best Orthodox views and left in silence such private views which have not tried to proclaim themselves the only Orthodox views.

I myself fear the cold hearts of the "intellectually correct" much more than any errors you might find in Augustine. I sense in these cold hearts a preparation for the work of

Antichrist (whose imitation of Christ must also extend to "correct theology"!); I feel in Augustine the love of Christ.

Forgive me for my frankness, but I think you probably welcome it. I have spoken from the heart, and I hope you will not pass this letter around so it can be put in various "files" and picked apart for its undoubted shortcomings.

May God preserve us all in His grace! Please pray for us.

With love in Christ,
Unworthy Hieromonk Seraphim

P.S. An important point I didn't specify in the letter above—the extreme criticism of Augustine shows such a lack of *trust* in the Orthodox Fathers and bishops of the past who accepted him as a Father (including the whole Orthodox West before the Schism). This lack of trust is a symptom of the coldness of heart of our times.

20th-century icon of Blessed Augustine, located at the St. Herman of Alaska Monastery, Platina, California.

II

The Heart of Blessed Augustine

BELOW are passages from Blessed Augustine's *Confessions* which Fr. Seraphim underlined in his copy of the book.* These passages reveal those qualities in Augustine which Fr. Seraphim most valued, showing Augustine to be a true Father of Orthodox piety and a profound teacher of repentance.

Our heart is restless, until it repose in Thee.

Oh! that I might repose on Thee! Oh! that Thou wouldest enter into my heart, and inebriate it, that I may forget my ills, and embrace Thee, my sole good! What art Thou to me? In Thy pity, teach me to utter it. Or what am I to Thee that Thou demandest my love, and, if I give it not, art wroth with me, and threatenest me with grievous woes? Is it then a slight woe to love Thee not? Oh! for Thy mercies' sake, tell me, O Lord my God, what Thou art unto me. Say unto my soul, I am thy salvation. So speak, that I may hear. Behold, Lord, my heart is before Thee; open Thou the ears thereof, and say unto my soul, I am thy salvation. After this voice let me haste, and take hold on

---

* *The Confessions of St. Augustine,* trans. Edward B. Pussey, D.D. (New York: Collier-Macmillan, 1961).

Thee. Hide not Thy face from me. Let me die—lest I die—only let me see Thy face.

Lord, cleanse me from my secret faults, and spare Thy servant from the power of the enemy. I believe, and therefore do I speak. Lord, Thou knowest. Have I not confessed against myself my transgressions unto Thee, and Thou, my God, hast forgiven the iniquity of my heart?

I disobeyed, not from a better choice, but from love of play, loving the pride of victory in my contests, and to have my ears tickled with lying fables, that they might itch the more; the same curiosity flashing from my eyes more and more, for the shows and games of my elders.

Deliver those who call not on Thee yet, that they may call on Thee, and Thou mayest deliver them.

Deadly pleasure ... lures us from Thee.

I saw not the abyss of vileness, wherein I was cast away from Thine eyes.

Thefts also I committed, from my parents' cellar and table, enslaved by greediness, or that I might have to give to boys.... And is this the innocence of boyhood? Not so, Lord, not so; I cry Thy mercy, O my God. For these very sins, as riper years succeed, these very sins are transferred from tutors and masters, from nuts and balls and sparrows, to magistrates and kings, to gold and manors and slaves, just as severer punishments displace the cane.

For it was my sin, that not in Him, but in His creatures—myself and others—I sought for pleasures, sublimities, truths, and so fell headlong into sorrows, confusions, errors.

I will now call to mind my past foulness, and the carnal corruptions of my soul; not because I love them, but that I may love Thee, O my God. For love of Thy love I do it; reviewing my most wicked ways in the very bitterness of my remembrance, that Thou mayest grow sweet unto me (Thou sweetness never failing, Thou blissful and assured sweetness); and gathering me again out of that my dissipation, wherein I was torn piecemeal, while turned from Thee, the One Good, I lost myself among a multiplicity of things.

And what was it that I delighted in, but to love, and be loved? But I kept not the measure of love, of mind to mind, friendship's bright boundary: but out of the muddy concupiscence of the flesh, and the bubblings of youth, mists fumed up which beclouded and overcast my heart, that I could not discern the clear brightness of love from the fog of lustfulness. Both did confusedly boil in me, and hurried my unstayed youth over the precipice of unholy desires.... I boiled over in my fornications, and Thou heldest Thy peace, O Thou my tardy joy!

Where was I, and how far was I exiled from the delights of Thy house, in that sixteenth year of the age of my flesh, when the madness of lust (to which human shamelessness giveth free license, though unlicensed by Thy laws) took the rule over me, and I resigned myself wholly to it?

To whom tell I this? not to Thee, my God; but before Thee to mine own kind, even to that small portion of mankind as may light upon these writings of mine. And to what purpose? That whosoever reads this, may think out of what depths we are to cry unto Thee. For what is nearer to Thine ears than a confessing heart, and a life of faith?

When that my father saw me at the baths, now growing towards manhood, and endued with a restless youthfulness, he, as already hence anticipating his descendants, gladly told it to my mother; rejoicing in that tumult of the senses wherein the world forgetteth Thee its Creator, and becometh enamoured of Thy creature, instead of Thyself, through the fumes of that invisible wine of its self-will, turning aside and bowing down to the very basest things.

I lusted to thieve, and did it, compelled by no hunger, nor poverty, but through a cloyedness of well-doing, and a pamperedness of iniquity. For I stole that, of which I had enough, and much better. Nor cared I to enjoy what I stole, but joyed in the theft and sin itself.

Now, behold, let my heart tell Thee what it sought there, that I should be gratuitously evil, having no temptation to ill, but the ill itself. It was foul, and I loved it; I loved to perish, I loved mine own fault, not that for which I was faulty, but my fault itself.

Fair were those pears, but not them did my wretched soul desire; for I had store of better, and those I gathered, only that I might steal. For, when gathered, I flung them away, my only feast therein being my own sin, which I was pleased to enjoy. For if aught of those pears came within my mouth, what sweetened it was the sin.

Thus doth the soul commit fornication, when she turns from Thee, seeking without Thee, what she findeth not pure and untainted, till she returns to Thee.

Thou hast melted away my sins as if they were ice.

Whosoever, called by Thee, followed Thy voice, and avoided those things which he reads me recalling and confessing of myself, let him not scorn me, who being sick, was cured by that Physician, through whose aid it was that he was not, or rather was less, sick: and for this let him love Thee as much, yea and more; since by Whom he sees me to have been recovered from such deep consumption of sin, by Him he sees himself to have been preserved from the like consumption of sin.

I sank away from Thee, and I wandered, O my God, too much astray from Thee my stay, in these days of my youth, and I became to myself a barren land.

I loved not yet, yet I loved to love, and out of a deep-seated want, I hated myself for wanting not. I sought what I might love, in love with loving, and safety I hated, and a way without snares. For within me was a famine of that inward food, Thyself, my God.

To love then, and to be beloved, was sweet to me; but more, when I obtained to enjoy the person I loved, I defiled, therefore, the spring of friendship with the filth of concupiscence, and I beclouded its brightness with the hell of lustfulness; and thus foul and unseemly, I would fain, through exceeding vanity, be fine and courtly. I fell headlong then into the love wherein I longed to be ensnared. My God, my Mercy, with how much gall didst Thou out of Thy great goodness besprinkle for me that sweetness? For I was both beloved, and secretly arrived at the bond of enjoying; and was with joy fettered with sorrow-bringing bonds, that I might be scourged with the iron burning rods of jealousy, suspicions, and fears, and angers, and quarrels.

In the ordinary course of study, I fell upon a certain book of Cicero, whose speech almost all admire, not so his heart. This book of his contains an exhortation to philosophy, and is called "Hortensius." But this book altered my affections, and turned my prayers to Thyself, O Lord; and made me have other purposes and desires.

How did I burn then, my God, how did I burn to re-mount from earthly things to Thee, nor knew I what Thou wouldest do with me? For with Thee is wisdom. But the love of wisdom is in Greek called "philosophy," with which that book inflamed me.

And since at that time (Thou, O Light of my heart, knowest) Apostolic Scripture was not known to me, I was delighted with that exhortation, so far only, that I was thereby strongly roused, and kindled, and inflamed to love, and seek, and obtain, and hold, and embrace not this or that sect, but wisdom itself whatever it were; and this alone checked me thus unkindled, that the name of Christ was not in it. For this name, according to Thy mercy, O Lord, this name of my Saviour Thy Son, had my tender heart, even with my mother's milk, devoutly drunk in and deeply treasured; and whatsoever was without that name, though never so learned, polished, or true, took not entire hold of me.

I resolved then to bend my mind to the holy Scriptures, that I might see what they were.... For not as I now speak, did I feel when I turned to those Scriptures; but they seemed to me unworthy to be compared to the stateliness of Tully: for my swelling pride shrunk from their lowliness, nor could my sharp wit pierce the interior thereof. Yet were they such as would grow up in a little one. But I disdained to be a little one; and, swollen with pride, took myself to be a great one.

She [my mother], by that faith and spirit which she had from Thee, discerned the death wherein I lay, and Thou heardest her, O Lord; Thou heardest her, and despisedst not her tears, when streaming down, they watered the ground under her eyes in every place where she prayed; yea Thou heardest her. For whence was that dream whereby Thou comfortedst her; so that she allowed me to live with her, and to eat at the same table in the house, which she had begun to shrink from, abhorring and detesting the blasphemies of my error?

He [a certain Bishop] answered, that I was yet unteachable, being puffed up with the novelty of that heresy, and had already perplexed divers unskillful persons with captious questions, as she had told him: "but let him alone awhile" (saith he), "only pray God for him, he will of himself by reading find what that error is, and how great its impiety...." "Go thy ways and God bless thee, for it is not possible that the son of these tears should perish." Which answer she took (as she often mentioned in her conversations with me) as if it had sounded from heaven.

For this space of nine years (from my nineteenth year to my eight-and-twentieth) we lived seduced and seducing, deceived and deceiving, in divers lusts; openly, by sciences which they call liberal; secretly, with a false-named religion; here proud, there superstitious, everywhere vain.

Let the arrogant mock me, and such as have not been, to their soul's health, stricken and cast down by Thee, O my God; but I would still confess to Thee mine own shame in Thy praise.

And Thou, O God, from afar perceivedst me stumbling in that slippery course, and amid much smoke sending out some sparks of faithfulness, which I showed in that my guidance of such as loved vanity, and sought after leasing, myself their companion. In those years I had one, not in that which is called lawful marriage, but whom I had found out in a wayward passion, void of understanding; yet but one, remaining faithful even to her; in whom I in my own case experienced what difference there is betwixt the self-restraint of the marriage-covenant, for the sake of issue, and the bargain of a lustful love, where children are born against their parents' will, although, once born, they constrain love.

At this grief [over the death of a dear friend] my heart was utterly darkened; and whatever I beheld was death. My native country was a torment to me, and my father's house a strange unhappiness; and whatever I had shared with him, wanting him, became a distracting torture. Mine eyes sought him everywhere, but he was not granted them; and I hated all places, for that they had not him; nor could they now tell me, "he is coming," as when he was alive and absent. I became a great riddle to myself, and I asked my soul, why she was so sad, and why she disquieted me sorely: but she knew not what to answer me.... Only tears were sweet to me, for they succeeded my friend, in the dearest of my affections.

May I learn from Thee, who art Truth, and approach the ear of my heart unto Thy mouth, that Thou mayest tell me why weeping is sweet to the miserable?

Wretched I was; and wretched is every soul bound by the friendship of perishable things; he is torn asunder when he loses them, and then he feels the wretchedness which he had ere yet he lost them.

But in me there had arisen some unexplained feeling, too contrary to this, for at once I loathed exceedingly to live and feared to die.

To Thee, O Lord, it [my soul] ought to have been raised, for Thee to lighten; I knew it; but neither could nor would; the more, since, when I thought of Thee, Thou wert not to me any solid or substantial thing. For Thou wert not Thyself, but a mere phantom, and my error was my God.

THE HEART OF BLESSED AUGUSTINE

Blessed whoso loveth Thee, and his friend in Thee, and his enemy for Thee. For he alone loses none dear to him, to whom all are dear in Him who cannot be lost. And who is this but our God, the God that made heaven and earth, and filleth them, because by filling them He created them?

Whithersoever the soul of man turns itself, unless toward Thee, it is riveted upon sorrows, yea though it is riveted on things beautiful.

... O my soul, at least now thou art tired out with vanities. Entrust Truth, whatsoever thou hast from the Truth, and thou shalt lose nothing; and thy decay shall bloom again, and all thy diseases be healed, and thy mortal parts be reformed and renewed, and bound around thee: nor shall they lay thee whither themselves descend; but they shall stand fast with thee, and abide forever before God, Who abideth and standeth fast forever.

If bodies please thee, praise God on occasion of them, and turn back thy love upon their Maker; lest in these things which please thee, thou displease. If souls please thee, be they loved in God: for they too are mutable, but in Him are they firmly stablished; else would they pass, and pass away. In Him then be they beloved; and carry unto Him along with thee what souls thou canst, and say to them, "Him let us love, Him let us love: He made these, nor is He far off.... Descend, that ye may ascend, and ascend to God, for ye have fallen, by ascending against Him." Tell them this, that they may weep in the valley of tears, and so carry them up with thee unto God; because out of His spirit thou speakest thus unto them, if thou speakest, burning with the fire of charity.

But that orator was of that sort whom I loved, as wishing to be myself such; and I erred through a swelling pride, and was tossed about with every wind, but yet was steered by Thee, though very secretly.

I was then some six or seven and twenty years old when I wrote those volumes; revolving within me corporeal fictions, buzzing in the ears of my heart, which I turned, O sweet truth, to thy inward melody, meditating on the "fair and fit," and longing to stand and hearken to Thee, and to rejoice greatly at the Bridegroom's voice, but could not; for by the voices of mine own errors, I was hurried abroad, and through the weight of my own pride, I was sinking into the lowest pit.

I loved to excuse it [my sin], and to accuse I know not what other thing, which was with me, but which I was not. But in truth it was wholly I, and mine impiety had divided me against myself: and that sin was the more incurable, whereby I did not judge myself a sinner.

To Milan I came, to Ambrose the Bishop, known to the whole world as among the best of men, Thy devout servant; whose eloquent discourse did then plentifully dispense unto Thy people the flour of Thy wheat, the gladness of Thy oil, and the sober inebriation of Thy wine. To him was I unknowing led by Thee, that by him I might knowingly be led to Thee.

And while I opened my heart to admit "how eloquently he spake," there also entered "how truly he spake"; but this by degrees.

I determined therefore so long to be a Catechumen in the Catholic Church, to which I had been commended by my parents, till something certain should dawn upon me, whither I might steer my course.

Thou hadst made me wiser, yet did I walk in darkness, and in slippery places, and sought Thee abroad out of myself, and found not the God of my heart; and had come into the depths of the sea, and distrusted and despaired of ever finding truth.

She [my mother] found me in grievous peril, through despair of ever finding truth.

But that man [Ambrose of Milan] she loved as an angel of God, because she knew that by him I had been brought for the present to that doubtful state of faith I now was in, through which she anticipated most confidently that I should pass from sickness unto health, after the access, as it were, of a sharper fit, which physicians call "the crisis."

Nor did I yet groan in my prayers, that Thou wouldest help me; but my spirit was wholly intent on learning, and restless to dispute.

But as it happens that one who has tried a bad physician, fears to trust himself with a good one, so was it with the health of my soul, which could not be healed but by believing, and lest it should believe falsehoods, refused to be cured; resisting Thy hands, Who hast prepared the medicines of faith, and hast applied them to the diseases of the whole world, and given unto them so great authority.

None can be continent unless Thou give it; and that Thou wouldest give it, if with inward groanings I did knock at Thine ears, and with a settled faith did cast my care on Thee.

She [my mother] could, she said, through a certain feeling, which in words she could not express, discern betwixt Thy revelations, and the dreams of her own soul.

Many of us friends conferring about, and detesting the turbulent turmoils of human life, had debated and now almost resolved on living apart from business and the bustle of men; and this was to be thus obtained; we were to bring whatever we might severally procure, and make one household of all; so that through the truth of our friendship nothing should belong especially to any; but the whole thus derived from all, should as a whole belong to each, and all to all. We thought there might be some ten persons in this society.... But when we began to consider whether the wives, which some of us already had, others hoped to have, would allow this, all that plan, which was being so well moulded, fell to pieces in our hands, was utterly dashed and cast aside.

To Thee be praise, glory to Thee, Fountain of mercies. I was becoming more miserable, and Thou nearer. Thy right hand was continually ready to pluck me out of the mire, and to wash me thoroughly.

III

Standard Description of Blessed Augustine

"St. Augustine, Bishop of Hippo:

"St. Augustine was born in Tagaste in the province of Numidia in A.D. 354. His pious mother Monica tried to give him a Christian education. Although he was gifted with a cheerful and talented mind, in his youth he was reluctant to follow his mother's exhortations. He was already of a mature age when he was baptized by St. Ambrose of Milan. After his mother's death, he distributed all his wealth to the poor, embraced monasticism, and for three years labored in solitude and severe struggles. In 391, Valerian, Bishop of Hippo, ordained him to the priesthood (against his will), and in 395 Valerian insisted that Augustine be consecrated his vicar bishop. Valerian died and Augustine continued for 35 years to be the most active pastor of Hippo. With his sermons and writings he defeated the heretic Pelagius.

"St. Augustine died peacefully on August 28, 430, in the 76th year of his life. He was a great teacher and fruitful writer of the church, as he was called at the Seventh Ecumenical Council.

"(Based on the Greek Menaion, and *Historical Teaching of the Fathers of the Church,* by Philaret, Archbishop of Chernigov, vol. 3, p. 18)."*

---

* *Myesyatsoslov [Menaion] of the Orthodox Catholic Church,* compiled by Ivan Kosolapov, 2nd ed., in Russian (Simbirsk: I. G. Anychina, 1880), entry for June 15, p. 277.

IV

Service to our Father among the Saints
BLESSED AUGUSTINE
Bishop of Hippo

whose memory is celebrated on June 15

*Composed by Archimandrite Ambrose (Pogodin).
Commissioned by St. John (Maximovitch)
of Shanghai and San Francisco.*

VESPERS

We sing Blessed is the man: *the first antiphon.*

On Lord, I have cried: *6 stichera are sung.*

*Tone 8.
To the special melody:* O Most Glorious Wonder.

O holy Hierarch Augustine* thy life was in accordance with thy name.* Thou didst preach the greatness of God;* thou wast adorned with the greatness of deeds;* thou wast crowned with the greatness of struggles;* thou wast enlightened by the greatness of thy love towards Christ.* Wherefore pray for us who honor thee* that we be granted great mercy.

O holy Hierarch Augustine* though the land of Hippo is silent* we glorify thee as a conqueror of heresy,* as a confirmation of the Orthodox faith,* as a great praise of monastics,* as an adornment of hierarchs,* as one who loved to help the poor,* as an expounder of the Scriptures,* as a warm intercessor for us.* Pray that we be granted great mercy.

Having been bedewed with the divine words of Ambrose,* thou didst sprout forth ears of the virtues an hundredfold.* Thou art the beauty of the Church* and a burning lamp,* a flame that consumes heresies* and warms the hearts of the faithful.* Bishop of the city of Hippo,* O blessed Hierarch,* entreat now from Christ great mercy for those who honor thee.

Other stichera, Tone 2.
To the special melody: With what crowns of glory.

With what crowns of glory shall we crown the holy Hierarch,* the earthly angel and heavenly man,* the exceeding great Hierarch of the Church of Christ,* the Bishop of Hippo and adornment of the whole world,* who was filled with the love of Christ and lofty wisdom,* the expounder of doctrine and confirmation of the faith,* the honest instructor of monastics,* who was crowned by Christ our God,* Who hath great mercy.

With what honorable crowns will we glorify our instructor,* whose preaching has gone forth unto the whole world,* whose God-proclaiming lips were filled with the Spirit* and were not hidden by the oblivion of the grave;* but even now they speak forth mellifluous teachings* and show forth the good path to life,* crowned by Christ our God,* Who hath great and rich mercy.

With what crowns of adornment shall we crown the Hierarch,* the honorable praise of Ambrose the Great,* the graceful lamp of all the world,* most wondrous shepherd of the

Church,* the warm consolation of those in sorrow* and the unshaken confirmation of the wavering,* the firm opponent of Pelagius* and the final uprooter of heresies,* who was a vigilant zealot of the purity of the Church,* crowned by Christ our God,* Who hath great mercy.

Glory: Tone 6.

Come, ye multitude of monastics,* let us glorify our instructor* and honor his holy memory,* for he ever prays for us* who celebrate his all-honorable memory and cry out to him with love:* pray for us to the All-generous God,* for Whom thou didst ever work,* Whose field thou didst cultivate,* Whose sheep thou didst save,* Whose talent thou didst multiply,* to Whom, O holy Hierarch Augustine,* thou dost ever pray for our souls.

Both now: Dogmaticon, in the 6th Tone.

Who will not glorify thee, O Most Holy Virgin;* who will not hymn thy most pure giving of birth;* the Only-begotten Son, Who hath shone forth from the Father before the ages,* hath come also from thee, O Pure One,* unutterably incarnate,* being in nature God,* and having become in nature man for our sake,* not divided into two persons,* but made known in two natures without confusion,* to Him pray, O Pure and All-blessed One,* that there may be mercy on our souls.

Entrance. Prokeimenon of the day. Three Readings.

The Reading from the Book of Proverbs.
(Ch. 10:7, 6; 3:13–16)

THE MEMORY of the righteous man calleth forth for praises, and the blessing of the Lord is upon his head. Blessed is the man that findeth wisdom, and the man that getteth understanding. For the merchandise of it is better than the merchandise of silver, and the gain thereof than fine gold. She is more precious than costly stones; everything that is honored cannot be compared unto her. Length of days and years of life are in her right hand; and in her left hand riches and honor. Out of her mouth truth proceedeth, and law and mercy she carrieth on her tongue. Hear me, then, O children, for I will speak of excellent things; and happy is the man that will keep unto my ways, for my paths are the paths of life, and the desire is fashioned of the Lord. Wherefore I entreat you and put forth my voice before the sons of men, for with wisdom I set up everything; I have called forth counsel, understanding and knowledge. Counsel is mine and sound wisdom, mine is understanding and strength is mine. I love them that love me; and those that seek me shall find grace. Understand, then, O ye simple, the cunning, and ye uninstructed—direct your hearts unto it. Hearken unto me again, for I will speak of honorable things, and the opening of my mouth shall be of right things, for my mouth shall speak truth and wickedness is an abomination to my lips. All the words of my mouth are of righteousness; there is nothing forward or perverse in them. They are all plain to him that understandeth, and right to them that find knowledge. For I will teach you the truth, so that your hope may be in the Lord and ye may be with the Spirit.

The Reading from the Wisdom of Solomon.
(Ch. 6:12–16; 7:30; 8:2–4, 7–9, 21; 9:1–4, 10, 11, 13)

THE MOUTH of the righteous man bringeth forth wisdom, and the lips of the wise man know grace. The mouth of the wise man teacheth wisdom, and the truth delivereth from death. If a righteous man happeneth to die, hope is not lost, for the son of a righteous man is born unto life, and in his good things doth he acquire the fruit of righteousness. There is ever light unto the righteous and they obtain both grace and glory of the Lord; the tongue of the wise acknowledgeth the good, and in their hearts resteth wisdom. The Lord loveth the hearts of the righteous, and acceptable unto Him are all the undefiled in the way. The wisdom of the Lord doth illumine the countenances of the wise. She preventeth them that desire her, in making herself first known unto them. She is easily seen of them that seek her. Whosoever seeketh her early shall have no great travail; and whosoever watcheth for her shall quickly be without care. For she goeth about seeking such as are worthy of her, showing herself favorably unto them in the ways, and meeteth them in every thought. Vice shall never prevail against wisdom. Wherefore I was a lover of her beauty; I loved her, and sought her out from my youth. I desired to make her my spouse, yea, the Lord of all things Himself loved her. For she is privy to the mysteries of the knowledge of God and a lover of His works. Her labors are virtues, for she teacheth temperance and prudence, justice and fortitude; and which are such things, as men can have nothing more profitable in their life. If a man desire much experience, she knoweth things of old, and conjectureth aright what is to come. She knoweth the subtleties of speeches and can expound dark sentences; unto all she is a counselor of good things, since there is immortality in her, and she is a comfort in cares and grief. Wherefore I prayed unto the Lord, and besought Him, and with my whole heart I said: O God of my fathers, and Lord of mercy, who hast made all things with Thy word, and fashioned man in Thy wisdom that he should have dominion over the creatures which Thou has made, and ordered the world according to equity and righteousness! Give me wisdom that sitteth by Thy throne, and reject me not from among Thy children, for I am Thy servant and the son of Thine handmaid. O send her out of Thy holy heavens, and from the throne of Thy glory, that being present she may labor with me, that I may know what is pleasing unto Thee. And she shall lead me soberly in my doings and preserve me in her glory. For the thoughts of mortal men are miserable, and our devices are but uncertain.

The Reading from the Wisdom of Solomon.
(Ch. 4:10–12; 6:21; 7:15–17, 22, 26, 29; 2:1, 10–17, 19–22)

WHEN the righteous man is praised the people rejoice, for his memory is undying, since he is acknowledged both of God and man, and his soul pleased the Lord. Love, therefore, O ye men, wisdom, and ye shall live; desire her and ye shall be instructed, for the very beginning of her is love and the keeping of the law. Honor wisdom, that ye may reign forevermore. I will tell you and will not hide God's mysteries from you, for He it is that leadeth unto wisdom and directeth the wise; in His hands is all wisdom and knowledge of workmanship; and wisdom, which is the worker of all things, will teach you all, for in her is a spirit understanding and holy, brightness of everlasting light, and an image of the goodness of God. She maketh people friends of God and prophets, she is more beautiful than the sun, and above all order of stars; being compared with the light, she is found before it. She hath freed from diseases those that pleased her, and hath set them in the right paths; she hath given unto them understanding to keep in holiness, saved them from those lying in wait, and granted them strength of power, so that all may understand that the most powerful of all is piety, and that vice shall never prevail against wisdom, nor shall judgment pass away without convicting the evil. But the ungodly, reasoning with themselves not aright, said: let us oppress the righteous man, let us not spare the widow, neither need we be ashamed of the ancient hairs of the aged. Let our strength be the law, and let us lie in wait for the righteous, because he is not of our turn, and he is clean contrary to our doings; he upbraideth us with our offending the law and objecteth to our infamy the transgressions of our education; he professeth to have the knowledge of God, and he calleth himself the child of the Lord. He was made to reprove our thoughts; he is grievous to us even to behold, for his life is not like other men's, his ways are of another fashion; we are esteemed of him as counterfeits, he abstaineth from our ways as from filthiness, he pronounceth the end of the just to be blessed. Let us see if his words be true, let us prove what shall happen in the end of him. Let us examine him with despitefulness and torture, that we may know his meekness and prove his patience; let us condemn him unto a shameful death, for by his own saying he shall be respected. Such things did they imagine and were deceived, for their own wickedness hath blinded them. As for the mysteries of God, they knew them not, neither did they discern that Thou art the Only God that hast the power of life and death, that savest in the time of tribulation and deliverest from every evil, that Thou art compassionate and merciful, granting to the just Thy grace, and setting Thy might against the haughty.

Aposticha, Tone 4.

He Who appeared in the garden to Mary* and banished from her wailing and tears,* the Same appeared unto thee in a garden* and commanded thee to open the Scripture and read it,* and reading it thou wast shown a wondrous path of life.* Pray to Christ God that we also follow it* that we may be guided to the Kingdom of Heaven.

Verse: Thy priests shall be clothed with righteousness // and Thy righteous shall rejoice.

Thy mother did greatly weep* when she saw thee perishing in the mire of sin,* and she diligently prayed that thou wouldst be saved.* And God inclined His ear to her prayer,* for it was not possible for the fruit of such prayer to perish.* Therefore, having been instructed by divine words* thou didst finally step away from the broad path* and didst follow the path of monastic struggle* and wast revealed as the summit of hierarchs,* a treasury of divine teachings,* a spiritual flute,* a supreme mystical embodiment of doctrines,* and the boast of the Church of Christ.

Verse: The saints shall boast in glory // and they shall rejoice upon their beds.

Having gathered a spiritual treasure* thou didst scatter thy worldly treasures to those in need.* Kissing voluntary slavery* thou didst receive the monastic rank* and wast a model for hierarchs and a rule for monastics,* a standard of virtue and a cup filled with love,* an unshakable rock of faith* and a most goodly teacher of meekness.* O Augustine, blessed father, pray for our souls.

Glory, Tone 5.

Tagaste is glorified by thy birth* and Madaura and Carthage are magnified in thee.* Rome is filled with joy through thee,* but even more is Milan adorned by thee,* for there wast thou born in spirit.* The great see of Hippo has thee as its bishop and good shepherd.* The whole world honors thee as a good teacher and a strong leader* and fervent intercessor for our souls.

Both now: in the same tone.

All-hallowed Virgin,* thou art the Temple and the Gate,* the Palace and the Throne of Kings.* Christ the Lord Who is my Deliverer* appeared through thee to those asleep in darkness,* because He, the Son of Righteousness,* wished to give light to the work of His hands* fashioned in His own image:* as thou hast the boldness of a mother towards thy Son,* we entreat thee whom all men sing,* beg Him to save our souls.

TROPARION, Tone 4.

Today the whole inhabited earth rejoices and radiantly celebrates thy memory, thou who hast trampled down heresy and confirmed Orthodoxy, and who hast given drink to the hearts of the faithful with the river of thy words, O servant of the Most Holy Trinity and inextinguishable lamp of the Church. O holy Hierarch Augustine, entreat Christ God that our souls be saved.

Glory, Both now: Theotokion in the same Tone.

The mystery hidden from the ages* and unknown to angels,* through thee, O Mother of God, is revealed to those on earth:* God incarnate in unfused union,* and accepting the Cross voluntarily for our sake,* by which, having raised first-created man,* He hath saved our souls from death.

MATINS

On God is the Lord: *Troparion to the Saint, twice.*
Glory, Both now: The mystery hidden from the ages.

Sessional hymn after the first kathisma, Tone 4.

Gather together ye multitude of monks,* in memory of our holy Hierarch,* and let us give him reverence with honorable hymns,* and even more so let us glorify him by our lives.* He seeketh the salvation of his children* and is revealed as a fervent supplicator on behalf of those who honor his memory.* May no one fall away from the blessed one.* May no one give himself over to the path of destruction.* May no one be careless about his salvation,* for we are all the children of the blessed Hierarch.

Glory, Both now: Theotokion.

How may I worthily hymn thee?* How may I glorify thee, O our Lady?* I am perplexed and amazed.* I fear to have boldness but am afraid to be negligent;* however, accept our praise with thy usual loving-kindness* and send down rich mercy to those who hymn thee.

Sessional hymn after the second kathisma, Tone 1.

O spiritual orator, instructor of Orthodoxy,* holy Hierarch Augustine, we all praise thee.* Thou didst smite heresy and save Christ's flock, O good one.* Thou didst lead countless people to the heavenly mansions,* and thou dost now gush forth healings to those who celebrate thy memory with faith.

Glory, Both now: Theotokion.

The Archangel Gabriel brought unto thee the greeting, "Rejoice,"* but what shall we on earth offer thee?* How can we chant a worthy hymn?* How can we praise thee or how can we glorify thee?* What manner of thanksgiving can we offer?* But, according to thy word we glorify thee, crying out as we are accustomed to do:* Rejoice, thou who art full of grace, the Lord is with thee.

After the polyeleos, Sessional hymn, Tone 3.
To the special melody: "To the beauty of Virginity."

Contemplating with thy sight heavenly beauty and earthly goodness,* thou didst cleave with all thy heart to the Creator of all,* and thou didst desire Him alone.* Therefore, having given away thy possessions to the poor, * thou didst acquire spiritual riches,* and wast a skillful monk, a hierarch and a great treasury of teaching.

Glory, Both now: Theotokion.

We sing hymns to thee, O Theotokos Virgin* Who didst deliver us from our forefather's curse and didst lead the human race to Paradise.* And we, thy slaves, ever pray to thee:* Entreat the All-generous God* that He may grant remission of sins and salvation from misfortunes and temptations* to those who hymn thee faithfully.

Hymns of degrees, first antiphon of Tone 4.

Prokeimenon, Tone 4.

My mouth shall speak wisdom and the meditation of my heart shall be of understanding.

Verse: The mouth of a just man reflects wisdom.

The Reading from the Holy Gospel according to St. John. (Ch. 10:9–16)

After the 50th Psalm, Sticheron, Tone 6.

Come and honor the memory of the Hierarch,* crying out to him faithfully:* O holy Hierarch Augustine,* great praise of the Church,* most wondrous instructor of all the world,* true teacher of monks.* Thou who art now standing before the throne of Christ God,* look down upon us thy children* and do not abandon us who love thee,* but cry out to us against those who war with us,* "I am with you and no one is against you."

SERVICE TO

Canon to the Theótokos, and this Canon to the Hierarch, Tone 4.

Acrostic: WE OFFER A CANON TO HIERARCH AUGUSTINE.

CANTICLE I

Irmos: I shall open my mouth …

Refrain: Holy Hierarch Augustine, pray to God for us.

We celebrate thy solemnity today, O blessed Hierarch. Remember us in thy holy prayers, that we might henceforth set aside worldly care and the path that leadeth to destruction, and direct our steps to the Kingdom of God.

Ever bearing the name of greatness, thou didst clearly impress the greatness of the Most Holy Trinity upon thy soul and, as much as thou wast able, didst express at length the hidden mysteries thereof. Pray to the Holy Trinity that the great multitude of our sins be forgiven us.

Glory.

O Father Augustine, thou didst clearly preach so that what is unapproachable to the corruptible mind may be gazed at through faith. Thou didst thunder forth apostolically to the ends of the inhabited earth, shining with the lightning of doctrine. Entreat thou for us who honor thee, spiritual enlightenment and great mercy.

Both now.

Fitly do we hymn thee, O Ever-Virgin, praise of our race. Through thee did God come and dwell with us, that He might save man from sin, and having saved him, might glorify him by His Divinity and might deify him through the gift of His grace. Therefore we all magnify thee.

Katavasia: same as Irmos.

CANTICLE III

Irmos: O Mother of God, thou living and plentiful fount ...

First Hippo had thee as an honorable luminary, but now the whole world is glorified by the beauty of thy memory, O Augustine. Thou wast a fortress of Orthodoxy and confirmation of the Church, a rule of life and a most honorable law of virtue.

Even the oblivion of the grave did not overshadow thy lips, O intercessor. Hippo is silent, Carthage is turned to dust, the glory of this world hath disappeared; but the whole inhabited earth speaks of thy great works and of thy struggles for Orthodoxy, and the Church of God sends up praise to thee with thanksgiving.

Glory.

Resting in divine delight, thou didst reject everything else as dung; having distributed thy corruptible riches to the poor, thou didst acquire an eternal heavenly treasure; and, leaving thy relations, thou wast joined to the choir of heavenly intercessors.

Both now.

As we honor thee with love we glorify thee, O Mother of God, most beautiful flower of incorruptible paradise, crown of unfading chastity, great throne of the Almighty, glory of the Christian race and wonder of the angels.

Sessional hymn, Tone 8.

Filled with divine wisdom, thou didst proclaim the honorable teaching of the Church,* offering confirmation of doctrine and expounding the Divine Scripture,* honoring in words the memory of the saints,* setting forth a rule for monastics both by thy life and by thy writings.* Wherefore thou didst ascend to the heights of theology* and, like Moses, having struck the hidden and unapproachable rock of theology with the staff of divine faith,* thou didst cause to gush forth a fountain of water flowing to life eternal—thy mellifluous words,* which thou didst give to drink in abundance for thirsting people.* Wherefore we cry out to thee, O our holy Hierarch Augustine,* pray to Christ God that remission of sins be granted to those who honor thy holy memory with love.

Glory, Both now: Theotokion.

As a Virgin and alone among women thou didst, without seed, give birth to God in the flesh.* Thou art glorified by the whole human race.* The fire of divinity dwelt within thee and thou didst feed the Creator and Lord with milk as an Infant.* Therefore the races of Angels and men worthily glorify thy most holy Birthgiving and harmoniously cry out to thee:* Pray to Christ God that remission of sins be granted to those who with faith venerate thy most holy Birthgiving.

CANTICLE IV

Irmos: He who sits in glory ...

Condemning the foolish and unruly Manichaeans, thou didst

scatter their false teachings like dust by the wind of thy divine teachings, and thou didst lay low the pride of Pelagius and didst lead the assembly of the Donatists to the Orthodox faith, O Augustine.

Although thou hast bodily left thy children, O all-beloved one, thou hast not abandoned us in spirit, who honor thee and thine honorable works as pearls of great price. By thy prayers thou visitest those who faithfully honor thy memory, O Blessed Augustine.

Glory.

Named as Bishop by Hierarch Valerian, thou wast regarded by him as a son. When he reposed thou didst accept the episcopate of Hippo and didst labor there without sloth for thirty-five years, teaching and admonishing and presenting thyself to all as an image of perfect virtue.

Both now.

O our praiseworthy Lady, most pure Ever-Virgin Theotokos, hearken unto us in our last hour and save us, praying diligently for us together with the holy Hierarch. And be merciful to us in the hour of judgment, and free us speedily from various calamities.

CANTICLE V

Irmos: The whole world was amazed at Thy divine glory ...

Nigh unto the enslavement of thy city by barbarians, God heard thy prayer, O holy one, and took thee to Himself, granting thee a crown of glory, as a good shepherd, as a zealous worker in Christ's vineyard, as a faithful servant who multiplied well the talent of thy Lord.

Thou didst expound the mysteries of the Holy Scripture and didst love above all the Gospel of St. John and his first Epistle, and didst clearly explain the Savior's Sermon on the Mount, and didst adorn the Psalms of David with thy holy commentary, O divinely wise father.

Glory.

Observing in thyself the mystery of the love of God, thou didst tell us not to take rest in our spirit until we have found repose in God. Having found it thyself, pray that we may find that peace both now and unto the ages.

Both now.

He who runneth to thy protection, O Lady, speedily findeth rest from sins and from life's problems. Therefore, cover with thine omophorion us who run to thee, and save us, O fervent Helper of Christians.

CANTICLE VI

Irmos: As we celebrate this sacred and solemn feast …

In admonishing for three days the bishops who fell away from the Orthodox faith, thou didst enlighten them by thy divine preaching. Wherefore, rejecting false teaching, they zealously embraced Orthodoxy and thou didst become known as a leader of those who are saved.

Educating people to honor and embrace humble virginity, thou didst also praise honorable marriage and didst instruct widows to preserve themselves. Thou wast doubly assiduous concerning abstinence, teaching thy disciples to follow and be saved by it, O thrice-blessed father.

Glory.

Rome boasteth of thy studies, Tagaste of thy childhood years, Carthage of thy youth, and Milan of thy repentance; but above all is the city of Hippo glorified by thee, as its blessed shepherd and honorable bishop.

Both now.

Archangel Gabriel, standing before the Virgin in Nazareth, announced the universal mystery, that God wished to be born of the Virgin, that He might renew mankind. Therefore thee, as participant in our salvation, do we ever magnify with love.

KONTAKION, Tone 2.

Holy Hierarch and theologian, boast of the Church of Christ, instructor of piety and confirmation of the Orthodox faith, uprooter of heresies, treasury of mystical teachings; blessed Father Augustine, most wondrous Hierarch, ever pray for us all.

Ikos: Enlighten the darkened eyes of my heart, O holy Hierarch and teach me to worthily hymn thy memory and send up the praise of thy wondrous life, which thou didst live angelically. Teach me to receive thy teachings with my heart and instruct me to travel the path of virtue and never to depart from the way that leadeth to eternal life. Show unto me that which I must think, say and do. Bind my hands and feet with the fear of God. Move me to the love of Christ, ever to strive and not be captivated by the corruptible beautiful things of this world, but strengthen me to seek without sloth the future treasures, ever praying for us all.

CANTICLE VII

Irmos: The holy children bravely trampled ...

Revealing thy sins and proclaiming thy love for the Lord as no one else hath done, thou didst say, O father: "I love my God, I regard all else as dust, Him alone do I seek, to Him alone do I wish to cleave."

Chosen for the honor of the episcopacy, thou wast a model for thy disciples, O blessed one, and didst remain unremittingly in monastic labors, adding to them further, ever struggling in vigils, prayer, fasts and labor, until thou becamest as an angel rather than a man.

Glory.

Having no alarm at the fall of ancient Rome, thou didst instruct Christians, O holy Hierarch. The City of God—the Church of Christ—shall never be destroyed, whose doctrine thou didst at length expound, and didst zealously call upon all believing and unbelieving people to be her children.

Both now.

Adam fell, having received in his ears the counsel of Eve, but he is saved by thee, O Maiden, and ever hymneth thee, crying out in joy: Rejoice, deliverance of our race; Rejoice, destruction of the serpent; Rejoice, most wondrous amendment of Eve.

CANTICLE VIII

Irmos: The offspring of the Theotokos saved ...

Unto the divine words of the great Ambrose didst thou

hearken, O father, and he instructed thee and taught thee to tread the good path of repentance. O worthy fruit of an honorable mother! O greatest disciple of a great teacher! Pray for our souls, O Father Augustine.

God, Who saved Paul on the road to Damascus, ensnared thee by an Epistle, saying, "Take and read." Having read it, thou didst abandon all things earthly as false and didst find Christ the Lord as the precious pearl of life eternal; and, not turning back, thou didst cleave to Him in love.

Glory.

Unfolding the teaching of being merciful by giving to those in need and by forgiving offenses, thou wast thyself a good instructor in this: Thou didst give away all thou hadst to the poor and didst acquire a wealth of meekness and an inexhaustible treasury of love, O venerable one.

Both now.

Save all who honor thee with love, O Mother of God, wealth of all good things, and be thou merciful to us who are in misfortune. Intercede for us who are in adverse circumstances and save us all, O all-hymned Virgin.

CANTICLE IX

Irmos: Let every mortal born on earth ...

Traversing the path of virtue, thou didst cry out to thy fellow travellers never to stop, proclaiming, "Say, 'it is enough,' and, behold, thou shalt perish. Be not depleted, brethren, nor enfeebled on your way to heaven." Help us also, O Hierarch, to ascend to Heaven.

Instructor by thy *Confessions,* most wondrous, honorable Hierarch, universal luminary, O Augustine, strengthen against the passions us who celebrate thy holy festival today. Help us in misfortunes, instruct us in the virtues and pray to the Lord that our souls may be saved.

Glory.

Now, as we pray to thee, O holy Hierarch, look down upon us form the height of Heaven and mercifully visit us. Thou seest the evil unbelief and the troubled waters on the sea of life. Hearken unto the cry of the ravaged churches, help us infirm ones, for thou hast boldness before the Lord as an honorable Hierarch.

Both now.

Ever-Virgin most pure, Mother of the Almighty, who didst open unto us the gates of life, look down upon us and shield us with thine honorable protection. Defend, O Lady, thine infirm children who place their hope in thee and who ever boast in thee.

Exapostilarion.

Come, let us glorify the holy Hierarch Augustine, as a good shepherd and a wise instructor, as a lamp of our Orthodox faith, as an intercessor for our souls.

Theotokion.

O Virgin boast of Christians, defender of the offended, strengthening of the enfeebled, healer of the infirm, speedy deliverer of those burdened by sins, save us who hope in thee.

Lauds, 4 stichera, Tone 4.
To the special melody: "What shall we call thee?"

What shall we call thee, O holy Hierarch? Adornment of the city of Hippo? But thou art the boast of the whole world. A man of honor? But by thy life thou wast an angel. A shining luminary? But thy light will never be extinguished. A voice that proclaimeth God? But thy voice hath not been silenced by the lid of the grave. Great are thy virtues, great are thy crowns with which Christ our God did crown thee. Pray that our souls be saved.

What shall we now call thee, O Augustine? Great Hierarch or glory of monastics; excellent shepherd or boast of fasters; powerful exposer of heresies or true instructor of meekness; namesake of virtue or rule of repentance; zealot of philosophy or glory of hermits; good lover of the poor or one who hath finally abandoned the world? Beauty of monastics, foundation of hierarchs, instructor of the love of wisdom; pray that our souls be saved.

What shall we name thee now, O Augustine? Beloved disciple of Ambrose the Great? But by the depth of thy repentance thou didst surpass him. Successor of the wondrous Valerian? But thou wast enlightened beyond him. Holy fruit of St. Monica? But thou wast sanctified beyond her, and didst ascend to the heights of heaven, where thou dost take delight in eternal joy. Pray that our souls be saved.

Proclaiming the City of God, whose great citizen thou wast, and an oracle of the mysteries of God, thou didst uphold the Orthodox Church, admonishing and teaching by thy deeds and words; and now thou hast set in the west like the sun, enlightening us by thy writings, teaching us to seek the grace of Christ and not to think highly of ourselves, but instead to be filled with the Spirit, of Whose breath thou wast an abundant partaker, being a mystic of theology. Pray that we may be saved.

Glory: Tone 6.

Who can worthily hymn thy labors, by which thou didst labor for the whole Church? Thou didst behead godless heresies with the sword of thy corrections, exposing the Arians, laying low the Manichaeans, leading the Donatists to the faith, breaking the audacity of Pelagius, and planting Orthodoxy. In gathering many children into the mansions of the Church, and instructing and guiding them, thou didst lead them into the heavenly mansions. Gather also us who are greatly scattered across the face of the earth and bring us to Christ our God, praying always to Him that our souls be saved.

Both now: in the same tone.

O Mother of God, thou art the true vine that hath brought forth for us the fruit of life. To thee we pray: pray, O Sovereign Lady, with the apostles and all the saints, that there may be mercy on our souls.

This service was composed by Archimandrite Ambrose Pogodin (upon the request of Archbishop John of Western Europe),* presented by His Eminence Archbishop John to the Synod of Bishops and approved by them to be used in churches.
                        Synodal Document of May 15, 1955 (o.s.).

---

* I.e., St. John (Maximovitch) of Shanghai and San Francisco. See pp. 79 and 93 above.—ED.

INDEX

Against Nestorius (St. John Cassian), 35, 52
Ambrose of Milan, St., 10 ill., 16, 18 ill., 20–21, 52, 69–70, 74, 76, 87, 112–113, 115, 118–119, 134, 137
Ambrose (Pogodin), Archimandrite, 117, 138
Anastassy, Metropolitan, 79
ancestral sin, 26, 28, *see also* original sin
Antichrist, 101
Apocalypse (St. John the Theologian), 81
Aquinas, Thomas, 70, 98
Arianism, 22
Arians, 137
asceticism, 34, 45
Augustine, Blessed
  as scapegoat, 25–26, 85, 99
  attitude of St. Faustus toward, 56
  attitude of St. Gregory the Dialogist toward, 61
  attitude of St. John Cassian toward, 52
  attitude of St. Photius the Great toward, 65–68
  attitude of the Orthodox Church toward, 14–16, 25, 30–31, 81, 94, 96, 98
  as combatter of chiliasm, 81
  commentaries on Scripture by, 61
  conversion of, 20, 89, 112
  correction of the errors of, 22, 37–42, 60
  errors of, 22, 28, 36, 38–40, 46, 48, 50, 59, 68, 71, 78, 93, 100
  as Father of Orthodox piety, 80, 100
  feast day of, 79
  iconographic features of, 81
  icons of, 4, 24, 82, 102
  service to, 117–138
  teaching on grace of, 33–42, 53, 60, 93
  teaching on the Holy Trinity of, 65–68
Augustine the Bishop (F. Van Der Meer), 80 n.
Augustinos (Kantiotes), Bishop of Florina, Greece, 8 ill., 9
Azkoul, Fr. Michael, 97

Basil the Great, St., 74, 78, 94
Beaucaire, France, 54

Caesarius of Arles, St., 59, 99
Call of All Nations, The (Prosper of Aquitaine), 54–55, 56 n.
Calvin, John, 49–50

INDEX

Carthage, 19, 124, 129, 132
Cefalu Cathedral, Sicily, 4
Celestine, Pope, 53
Chapel of St. Victor "of the Golden Sky," Milan, 18
chiliasm, 81
Cicero, 19, 107
City of God, The (Blessed Augustine), 16, 22
Commonitory (St. Vincent of Lerins), 45
Complete Works of I. V. Kireyevsky, 33 n.
Conferences (St. John Cassian), 34, 39, 42, 48, 57
Confessions (Blessed Augustine), 16–17, 20, 22, 77, 80, 85, 89, 96, 103, 103 n.
Council of Arles, 49
Council of Carthage, 22
Council of Florence, 69, 87
Council of Orange, 55–56, 60

Demetrius of Rostov, St., 28, 75
de Torquemada, Juan, Cardinal, 72
Dialogues (Plato), 20
Dialogues (St. Gregory the Great), 99
Dionysius of Alexandria, St., 71
Donatist Schism, 22, 130, 137
Dorotheos of Gaza, St., 95

Early Church, The (Henry Chadwick), 20 n.
Ecumenical Councils, 73
    Fifth, 61, 69, 71, 94
    Seventh, 116
    Third, 35
Elias of Egypt, ascetic, 86
Eustratius Argenti (Timothy Ware), 78, 78 n.

Faustus of Lerins, St., 56, 58–59, 75, 99
Faustus, St., Bishop of Rhegium, 49, 59
Filioque, 65, 67, 69
fools-for-Christ, 76
free will, 25, 33, 36–38, 40, 42, 45, 48, 55–59
Fulgentius of Ruspe, 47, 57
Gennadius of Marseilles, presbyter, 57, 59
    on grace and predestination, 57
Gennadius, disciple of St. Mark of Ephesus, 98
George of Zadonsk, Elder, 77
Gervasius, St., 21
Gottschalk, monk, 49
grace, 34, 53, *see also* Augustine, Blessed, teaching on grace of; prevenient grace
    and free will, 35-37, 39–40, 45–46, 48–49, 55–58
    controversy over, 33
    cooperation of, 40–41, 58
Grand Inquisitor, 72
Gregory of Nyssa, St., 71–72, 74, 76, 88, 93
Gregory of Sinai, St., 83
Gregory of Tours, St., 75, 95
Gregory Palamas, St., 64 ill., 67, 83
Gregory the Dialogist (the Great), St., 61, 75, 99
Gregory the Theologian, St., 76, 78, 87, 94
guilt, "original," 26

Hadrumetum, 34, 37
Hilarion, Archbishop of Sydney, 93 n.
Hilary of Arles, St., 38
Hilary of Poitiers, St., 51–52, 74, 87

INDEX

Hippo, 16, 118, 124, 128, 130, 132, 136

Historical Teaching of the Fathers of the Church (*Patrology*) (Archbishop Philaret of Chernigov), 34 n., 67 n., 81, 97, 116

Holy Fathers, 14, 30, 49–50, 66, 73, 80, 88, 96, 101

"Hortensius" (Cicero), 108

Igor (Kapral), Father, 93

Incarnation, doctrine of, 36, 52–53

Inquisition, Spanish, 72

Institutes (St. John Cassian), 34

Irenaeus of Lyons, St., 71

Jansenism, 38

Jerome, Blessed, 52, 74, 76, 79

John Cassian the Roman, St., 32 ill., 34, 36–41, 49, 51, 56–57, 59–60, 87, 94, 98
  monastery of St. Victor founded by, 54

John Chrysostom, St., 21–22, 70, 77, 87, 94

John (Maximovitch) of Shanghai and San Francisco, St., 28, 79, 93–94, 96, 117, 138
  veneration of Western Saints by, 29

Justinian, Emperor, 62
  letter of, 69

Kireyevsky, Ivan V., 33

Kontzevitch, Ivan M., 15

Ladder of Divine Ascent, The (St. John Climacus), 95

Lateran Library, Rome, 82

Lausiac History, The (Palladius), 95

Leporius of Hippo, presbyter, 35

Lerins Island (Vincent Barralis), 59 ill.

Lerins Monastery, 60

"Liturgical Theology of Fr. A. Schmemann, The" (Fr. Michael Pomazansky), 84 n.

Lives of Illustrious Men (Blessed Jerome), 57

Lucidus, presbyter, 48, 56, 58

Luther, Martin, 49

Macarius of Corinth, St., 83

Madaura, 124

Manichaeans, 16, 19, 130, 137

Marie-Manoël, Sr., 32

Mark of Ephesus, St., 28, 70–71, 73, 73 ill., 74, 76, 87, 98
  on purgatorial fire, 69, 72

Marseilles, France, 32, 54

Martin of Tours, St., 75

Milan, Italy, 18, 21, 124, 132

monasticism, 13, 16, 34, 36, 41, 74–75, 115

Monica, St. (mother of Blessed Augustine), 16, 19, 108–109, 113–115, 123, 137

Moreno, Nicholas, 95

Mount Athos, 15

Myesyatsoslov of the Orthodox Catholic Church (Ivan Kosolapov), 116 n.

Mystagogia (St. Photius the Great), 67

Nectarios of Pentapolis, St., 88

Nestorius, 35, 51

Nicodemus of the Holy Mountain, St., 27, 78, 83, 93, 96

Objections of Vincent, The, 46

"On the Character of European

INDEX

Civilization," (I.V. Kireyevsky), 33 n.
On Ecclesiastical Dogmas (Gennadius of Marseilles), 57
"On the Gift of Perseverance" (Blessed Augustine), 38, 45
"On the Grace of God and Free Will" (Prosper of Aquitaine), 39
"On the Grace of God and Free Will" (St. Faustus of Lerins), 56
On the Trinity (Blessed Augustine), 68, 70, 76
Origenists, 71
original sin, 25, 100, *see also* ancestral sin
Orthodox Christian Witness, 93
Orthodox Word, The, 25, 84 n.

paganism, 19, 22
Paisius (Velichkovsky), St., 83, 97
papal infallibility, 72
Patrick (father of Blessed Augustine), 19
Patrick of Ireland, St., 94–95
patristic revival, 83–86
Patrology (Archbishop Philaret of Chernigov), 97
Pelagianism, 22, 35–36, 38–39, 76
Pelagius, 26, 34–35, 51, 56, 115, 119, 130, 137
Philaret of Chernigov, Archbishop, 34, 36, 79–80, 97
Philaret of Moscow, Metropolitan, 83
Philokalia, 88
Photius and the Carolingians (Richard Haugh), 65 n., 67 n.
Photius the Great, St., 14, 28, 64 ill., 65–72, 75, 88, 98
  defense of Blessed Augustine by, 67
piety, Orthodox, 22, 80, 89, 100

predestinarianism, 56, 58
predestination, 43–50, 57
  in Calvinism, 43, 47, 49
prevenient grace, 38–39, 56, 58
Prosper of Aquitaine, 38–40, 51, 53, 57
Protasius, St., 21
purgatory, 69, 71

Rhône River, 55 ill.
Roman, St., disciple of St. John Cassian, 54
Rome, 82, 124, 132, 134
Russian Ascetics of the 18th and 19th Centuries (Bishop Nikodim), 77 n.

St. Herman of Alaska Monastery, 12 ill.
St. Mark of Ephesus and the Union of Florence (Archimandrite Ambrose Pogodin), 70 n.
St. Roman de l'Aiguille, Monastery of, 54–55 ills.
St. Tikhon of Zadonsk (Nadejda Gorodetzky), 77 n.
St. Victor, Monastery of, 32, 54
San Francisco, California, 13–14
"semi-pelagianism," 35
Seraphim (Rose), Fr., 7 ill., 13–16, 92 ill., 103
  defense of Blessed Augustine by, 14–15
  letters of, 93–101
Soliloquies (Blessed Augustine), 70, 77, 80
Source Book for Ancient Church History, A (J. C. Ayer), 60 n.
Study of Gregory Palamas, A (Rev. John Meyendorff), 68 n.
Symeon the New Theologian, St., 83

INDEX

synergy, 40, 42, 44, 48, 56, 58, 60

Tagaste, 132
Theodoret of Cyrrhus, Blessed, 76
Theodoritos, Fr., 93
Theophan the Recluse, Bishop, St., 26–27, 44
Tikhon of Zadonsk, St., 27, 77–78
Torquemada, Juan de, 72
Tours, France, 82
Treatise on Unleavened Bread (Eustratius Argenti), 78
Tully, 108

Unseen Warfare, 94

Valerian, Bishop of Hippo, 115, 130, 137
Varlaam Monastery, Meteora, Greece, 24
Vigilius, Pope of Rome, 62
Vincent of Lerins, St., 45–46, 51, 53, 94, 98
Vita Patrum (The Life of the Fathers) (St. Gregory of Tours), 95

Western influence, 26–27, 83–84, 86–88, 94–96, 98

Zwingli, Ulrich, 49

St. Herman Press

ST. HERMAN OF ALASKA BROTHERHOOD

For over four decades, the St. Herman Brotherhood has been publishing books of Orthodox Christian spirituality. Write for our free catalogue, featuring over fifty titles.

St. Herman Press
P. O. Box 70
Platina, CA 96076

Visit our website and order online from:
www.sainthermanpress.com